GEORGE MONSOOR
AND ROSE REA

DEFEND
★ ★ US IN ★ ★
BATTLE

The True Story of MA2 Navy

SEAL Medal of Honor Recipient

MICHAEL A. MONSOOR

HARPER HORIZON

The actions of the few dictate the fate of many.

—ALEXANDER THE GREAT

Motto of BUD/S class 250

CONTENTS

FOREWORD

Of all of the lessons that I learned during my tenure as navy secretary, the most enduring has been the recognition of the great range of human beliefs and behaviors. It is hard to comprehend what would drive men to fly airplanes into the World Trade Center and the Pentagon, killing thousands of innocents. At the same time, we are presented with individuals such as Michael Monsoor, who are willing to do whatever is needed to preserve the lives of others.

Much has been said of those of the "Greatest Generation" who saved our nation during World War II. It is hard today to grasp fully the commitment and motivation that enabled those men to storm the beaches of Normandy and Iwo Jima. For our country, it was a time of near universal recognition of the existential threat posed by fascism, which led to a national response with much of the American population serving in uniform. The entire nation was engaged.

The response to the challenges of the twenty-first century—exemplified by the attacks of 9/11—has been far more selective. We have an all-volunteer military that disproportionally comes from families and communities with a long history of service. The vast majority of the American population has little if any contact with those who serve, let alone those who serve in our elite special forces.

Michael Monsoor was an exemplary SEAL—a man of great integrity, a skilled warrior, and a loyal teammate. That loyalty led to his willingness to sacrifice his life for his teammates. As the Bible teaches us, "Greater love hath no man than this, that a man lay down his life for his friends" (John 15:13).

One of my objectives as secretary was to help develop and motivate the next generation of sailors and marines. Both the navy and marine corps have great traditions and heroes dating back to John Paul Jones. Unfortunately, it can be difficult for young men and women, brought up in the twenty-first century, to relate to heroes from the age of sail. However, we also have great contemporary heroes such as Michael Monsoor who exemplify the characteristics that we look for in our future personnel. I worked to ensure that the memory of Michael is preserved and that his story is told to our latest generation of sailors and marines. To that end, I am most pleased to see this book published, as it tells the story of Michael as a child, a man, and a SEAL. A life's story well worth telling.

To the readers of this book, you will find Michael's story to be defined by the values we all hold dear. I would hope that you also take notice of the way that Michael's parents, George and Sally, instilled these values in Michael. Theirs is a story of the impact that parents have upon their children. Lastly, please note the story of the Navy SEALs and the ethos that defines them, an ethos that elevates commitment to the mission and the team above all. Not surprisingly, Michael's BUD/S class adopted the motto (attributed to Alexander the Great) "The actions of the few dictate the fate of many." We all have much for which to thank Michael, Task Unit Bruiser, and all the special operators who have defended us so faithfully.

Dr. Donald C. Winter
Secretary of the Navy, 2006–2009

DEFEND

* ⋆ ⋆ US IN ⋆ ⋆ *

BATTLE

ONE

The sun scorched outside as the muscular and well-built warfighter fell to the ground. He instinctively raised his rifle to his shoulder and fired while simultaneously clutching his push-to-talk and keying up. "LT, this is K. I've been shot. I say again, this is K. I've been shot!"

As his transmission came through the radio, strings of distinct machine gun fire could be heard cracking in the background one after the other. On the opposite end of the radio, J. P. Dinnell knew exactly what and who that was. "That's a Mark 48; it's Mikey! Let's go right now . . . we've got their position," yelled J. P. as they rapidly maneuvered to support the element under fire. In that same moment, Michael and K. along with one other SEAL (SEa, Air, Land, commando) and their Iraqi partners were on the receiving end of a violent enemy ambush from almost a dozen insurgent fighters.

It was over a hundred degrees as the sun beat down on the city of Ramadi, Iraq, where only a few years before the street would have been filled with the noise of bustling shops, cars, and pedestrians all going about the day's business. Now the street was lined with destroyed cars and tattered buildings speckled here and there with the unmistakable divots of bullet impacts. In 2006, there were an estimated four to five thousand enemy fighters in Ramadi when the roughly forty-man special operations task unit from SEAL Team 3, Task Unit Bruiser, was sent to restore order. They were tasked with providing bounding sniper overwatch for army and marine units as they cleared through Ramadi one section of the city at a time. This tactic consists of movement from high ground to high ground just ahead and to the flank of a ground unit conducting clearance, in order to prevent the enemy from attacking. For TU Bruiser, there was no time to settle in; they had arrived just as the fighting season was picking up pace christening them with a firefight as soon as the first night in the country. For some of the men, it was their first time in combat, and to say the air felt heavy with intensity would have been immensely inaccurate. Fighting throughout the country at the time was so intense, with so many wounded, that service members lined up almost weekly to give blood for the injured. For TU Bruiser, the days were a blur of twenty-four- to seventy-two-hour combat operations in searing heat, followed by a regroup and refit at base to eat, sleep, check each other's gear, and prepare for the next insert, normally taking place just after darkness fell.

There was a loud burst of gunfire, and K. fell to the ground exposed in the street. He had taken a round to his right femur. The barrage of enemy gunfire continued to cascade toward him from multiple enemy positions, kicking up dust and sending ricochet and secondary frag of rock and concrete right at him. K. immediately returned fire but was unable to move quickly to cover because of the grievous injury to his leg. Within seconds of hitting the ground, K. heard a new weapon enter the chaos. Michael Monsoor, the automatic weapons (AW) gunner, broke from his cover position in an adjacent courtyard into the middle of the street. In that same moment, Michael sent a long burst of 7.62-millimeter rounds from his Mk 48 machine gun into enemy positions. Although carrying more than a hundred pounds of equipment, Michael deftly moved to where K. lay wounded and bleeding. He stood in front of him and used his lean frame and armor as a shield to protect K. from incoming enemy fire. This gave the wounded SEAL the reprieve he needed to continue to call for backup on his radio. Michael's technical acumen was apparent as he swiftly engaged and suppressed enemy positions with his Mk 48, affectionately known as "the pig" by warfighters as it is likened to holding on to an angry, squealing pig. Every second and every round mattered.

The other SEAL began to prepare K. to move while Michael engaged the ten to twelve enemy insurgents.

"Let's move!" the other SEAL shouted.

Michael grabbed K.'s drag handle on the top of his armor and began to pull him back to the courtyard while still firing his Mk 48.

K. looked up at Michael as he dragged him across the road, but the perspective was not what he expected. K. felt as if, for just a moment, he had left his body below. He looked down upon the scene. As Michael dragged him, the snaps and ricochet of the heavy volume of enemy fire continued to hit the ground around them. K. couldn't believe that not one round had found its intended target. Instantly, the light seemed to shift, then he saw them; two large, feathered wings wrapped from behind Michael and around the trio as they moved him out of the street. K. knew in that instant: they were not alone in the fight. Then . . . K. was again looking up at Michael. He could feel the pain and hear the gunfire. Dust filled the air and the sun beat down upon them as they moved.

Once back behind cover, the other SEAL began working on his injured teammate. The enemy fire picked up again just as Michael had finished reloading. Michael answered with a heavy volley into the enemy position.

J. P. and the rest of the squad along with their Iraqi partners joined the firefight minutes later. Lieutenant Seth Stone, the officer in charge (OIC) of Delta Platoon, was deep into radio comms providing situation updates to the chain of command, coordinating with units in other sectors, and facilitating the movement of the responding soldiers, marines, and Iraqi partners into the fight. He instructed them to secure the area and CASEVAC (casualty evacuation) K. and crew. HMMWVs (high-mobility multipurpose wheeled vehicles) covered main avenues while SEALs directed the .50-caliber turret gunners to fire on enemy positions. J. P. and the rest of the squad swiftly locked down the immediate area and moved to Michael, K., and the other SEAL. J. P. and the others grabbed K. and loaded him into the HMMWV as the other SEAL followed. Just as J. P. and Michael closed the HMMWV door and moved to join the Iraqi partner force, a voice came over the squawk box: "All SEALs are up. Get to the aid station now! Let's move!"

TWO

"Michael," George said as he looked down at his newborn son that his wife, Sally, held delicately in her arms. "We'll name him Michael."

"Michael," Sally repeated softly, exhausted, but elated to welcome her third child into the world, following his siblings, Sara and James.

Sally had been researching names for their children while she was pregnant and began looking up Lebanese and Middle Eastern names to honor her husband's heritage. As they discussed further, George told Sally he wanted names selected from the Old Testament. Sally liked that idea and had chosen Sara for their first daughter as she took the lead in naming her. George would choose the names for their sons.

As they gazed upon their second son in the bright hospital room with his inquisitive brown eyes looking right back at theirs, his matted dark hair contrasting his fresh, soft skin, George knew Michael was the right name for him. Sally wholeheartedly agreed.

He was named after Saint Michael the Archangel, who in the Old Testament cast out of heaven all of the fallen angels led by Lucifer and condemned them to eternity in hell. He was a soldier full of strength and feared nothing. It was a perfect fit.

The hospital staff performed their newborn well checks on little Michael and after some time had passed, the pediatrician walked into their room.

"Mrs. Monsoor, Michael has jaundice, which is why his skin has a yellowish tint. It's caused by an excess of the pigment bilirubin typically because of an obstruction of the bile duct. You will be discharged today, but we need to keep Michael and put him in an incubator until his bilirubin gets lower."

Sally looked back at the doctor. She'd heard what he was telling her, but before she could help herself, she blurted out, "Doctor, I'm not leaving my son."

The pediatrician thought for a few minutes, as he could see the unwavering determination in her eyes and that she was adamant about not leaving him. "Well, Mrs. Monsoor, we will let you take him home, but you have to agree to a set protocol of treatment in the home including sitting with him by the window in the sun for two to three hours a day. If you follow our instructions and he continues to improve, he will not need to stay or come back to the hospital."

"Thank you so much. I will. I will do everything you need!" Sally replied, full of relief that she would not be separated from her son. She did just that—she spent hours a day holding him by the window as the sun poured through allowing the bilirubin in Michael's blood to be more easily excreted in order to reach a normal, healthy level.

Michael continued to grow, and although he was small in stature, he was full of energy and exuberance. He faced another challenge ahead in his early years, however, and began to struggle with severe asthma. So much so that his parents would take turns checking on him in the middle of the night to make sure their son was still breathing. They had taken more trips to the ER than either would like to recall. This was enough to break a young spirit, but through it all, this indomitable little boy, day after day, fought to rid his body of this weakness. The mental toughness and fortitude that Michael gained from this endeavor at such a young age laid the foundation for all future obstacles he would endure. Whether he was holding his breath in the family pool with his three siblings or racing them back and forth in it, he never quit trying to strengthen his lungs. George remembers how Michael would emerge from the depths of the pool breathing so deeply, he'd almost pass out as he continued to push himself harder to increase the capacity of his ailing lungs.

As he grew older, he was often the target of bullying at school as well as on the playground, and he began to hate it. He felt profoundly for himself the effects of someone victimizing someone less able to defend themselves in order for them to gratify their own desires. Even in his youngest years, he was keenly aware of the injustice that took place.

One afternoon, when Michael was around nine or ten, his father took him to the racetrack to scout out some future horse prospects, as their family raced thoroughbreds at the time. When they arrived, George began to chat with the trainer and Michael ran off to play on the playset in the compound. As Michael played with the other children, George noticed three older boys pushing the other children around, including Michael. They made a show of it in an effort to demonstrate to all of the children that they were in charge. They took over the only three swings and refused to get off for any of the smaller and younger children to use. "Not your swing, it's mine now!" They taunted the younger kids. George called Michael back to him and looked at his tear-filled eyes.

"Come here, Mikeys. I know those kids are being bullies, but not every wrong is yours to right. There is not always justice in the world. Sometimes you just have to move on," George told Michael.

"Dad, what is justice?" Michael asked, his curiosity piqued upon hearing the new word.

"Justice is getting or giving what is deserved, whether it's reward or punishment, Mikeys," George responded to his son, whom he always called Mikeys when it was just the two of them.

George could see his son taking in his words, yet his son's question continued to cut through his thoughts as they headed to their seats to watch the horses race. He could see it in Michael's eyes that the issue was not resolved. After the action-packed race, they returned to the area where they met the trainer. George asked Michael to stay nearby and wait for him. But as soon as George was speaking with the trainer, Michael shot off to the playground with fire in his eyes. Those same boys were again back on the swings taunting the younger children. Michael ran straight up to them from behind and ripped each boy out of their swing one at a time. He then sprinted up the play structure and began to climb the ladder that led up to the rocket ship that had multiple layers of slides and ladders. He knew if he could get to the top, only one bully could get to him at a time, and sure enough, they chased right up after him and one by one, he kicked each boy backwards over and over as they tried to attack him. When he could no longer defend himself, he initiated his escape plan. He leaped through the top rocket opening down the slide and ran as fast as he possibly could back to his father. This time, with the biggest grin on his face and eyes sparkling with excitement. He knew he was safe with his father by his side, and he had executed his plan perfectly. George and Michael got into their car to head back home, and George glanced across at his son who sat in the passenger seat, victoriously grinning back at him. "Dad . . . I think that's justice."

———————

George and Sally raised their four children in an upscale neighborhood in Anaheim Hills, California, but when the economy took a turn for the worse, George moved into other business ventures to take care of his family. He relocated the family to Garden Grove, California. They settled in a diverse neighborhood with families of all income levels and ethnic backgrounds. It was a necessary decision, but it also taught Michael to recognize, embrace, and appreciate what he had. After a few weeks at his new school in Garden Grove, George asked Michael how it was going. He replied, "Dad, no one speaks English."

"That's okay, Michael, you'll make friends soon enough."

"I'm talking about the teachers, Dad."

Michael, mindful of the disparity between his old neighborhood and new, settled into his new school and made friends quickly. Every Christmas, his parents would find out that he had given away many of his Christmas gifts to his friends who needed things more than he did. Even though Michael liked nice things, it wasn't lost on him that certain friends were more in need than he was. It became such a well-known fact that George would ask Michael with a wink each Christmas,

"What do your friends want for Christmas this year, Michael?"

Michael loved Christmas and was always up to something to make it memorable for those he cared about. His mother, Sally, recalls with a smile on her face when Michael surprised his entire family. They were going through a less successful time, and their financial situation was tight. In turn, it was decided that they would not exchange gifts that Christmas.

When December 25 arrived and the Monsoor family awoke bright and early on Christmas morning, each family member found a gift waiting for them underneath a long, slender Italian cypress tree that was freshly cut and placed into a dirt-filled bucket that served as its pot. There was a handful of tinsel tossed onto the little green tree that gave it just a hint of sparkle, and five wrapped Christmas gifts sat below it with names written on each one from Michael. "He went through different items he had collected as a child and decided to share some of them with each of us," said George. "He gave me some special rocks he had collected, and I still have them to this day."

"We all burst out laughing," Sally said, "when we saw the tree he had cut down for us to celebrate Christmas morning. What he selected for each of us was so special and amusing at the same time. Michael found one of my scarves, a free scarf I had saved from the horse-racing track, and wrapped it up along with some of his collected trinkets. It was one of the most memorable Christmases we have ever had. My son brought so much joy to us all with his clever efforts!"

"We laughed even harder when we stepped outside after opening our gifts and noticed that one of our four cypress trees in the front yard was cut in half," George added.

Where before, two cypress trees lined each side of their front window, there now stood two on one side but only one and a half on the other. An eyesore to a passerby but a token of joy to the Monsoor family from that day forward.

THREE

"Faster, Dad, faster!" Michael cheered as George drove him down the road in his 1964 Pontiac GTO. It was a sheen red and as smooth as glass. Michael loved riding in it with his dad, and when he'd jump in, he'd be singing the song written about the car called "Little GTO" by Ronnie and the Daytonas.

"Little GTO, you're really looking fine, three deuces and a four-speed and a 389 . . ."

"Michael would grab on to the handle above the glove box," George said, "and he'd be giggling and telling me to 'Go!' as soon as he saw that the highway entrance ramp was clear of cars.

"Once it was clear, then I'd floor it."

Off shot Michael and his dad, the windows rolled down and the cool air streaming through on a sunshine-filled

Southern California afternoon. George pushed down on the gas pedal and increased the speed on the ramp.

"Dad, we're going a hundred miles an hour!" a gleeful Michael yelled.

George smiled back at him. "Give or take fifty, Mikeys."

He then began to ease off the gas pedal before he hit the freeway and started to coast and slow down. Michael liked to hear the wheels as George pushed the speed; the sound and smell of burning rubber absolutely thrilled Michael. The GTO had an incredible amount of power. George would move through the gears so rapidly that the tires would shriek under the torque as they tried to catch up to the pounding engine. He deftly took each curve with skillful precision as they cruised on the highway side by side. Michael stared out the window and watched the trees flying by. That was all he needed; he was hooked. It would set the stage for his love of speed and cars from that moment forward. It fascinated Michael's growing mind. He loved the mechanics of the vehicle, the aerodynamics, and the beauty of the design of each car he and his dad explored. Plus, he loved the speed. He was always asking to go faster. It gave him an exhilaration and a rush of adrenaline unlike anything else, and he liked it. He thrived off of it.

Michael went on to push the limits in everything he did. George remembers watching Michael ride his bicycle over and over again up an incline formed from broken boards and anything he could get his hands on set against a curb. He would pedal as fast as he could as he approached the incline in an attempt to jump higher and farther. Michael did it again and again without any regard for what might happen if he fell.

He was always up for an adventure and brightened those around him with his half-cocked smile that seemed devious yet genuine at the same time. His affinity for high-thrill sports also fostered a love for street hockey. For a Southern California boy, that wasn't quite the norm, but he loved playing the sport. He'd strap on his old-school rollerblades just like the kids in *The Mighty Ducks* and head down the block to the local school park where thirty or so boys from the neighborhood would begin at daytime and play until their parents would come to get them for dinner.

The games would happen every single day during the summer, and this was, one of his closest childhood buddies, Scott Reynolds, recalls, their "sandlot" childhood. They stood up for themselves, they challenged each other, they played hard, and most important, they had a blast. Both Scott and Michael went on to play ice hockey as they got older, and more than once, he remembers Michael taking matters into his own hands when he'd come into contact with an opponent that thought it was no big deal to cheat or take cheap shots during the games. Scott would come out to the parking lot after the game to find Mike having fisticuffs with the guys who cheated. And often, Scott would jump in determined not to let his buddy take them on himself.

Lazy summer days of surfing and bodyboarding at Huntington Beach with Scott or his brothers turned into competitive sports nights as each boy grew older, stronger, and more athletic. Football and hockey were their sports of choice, and although they went to different schools, they always found time to connect, whether at their local Catholic church or catching the latest HBO fight at a friend's house. The loyalty of Michael's friendship was not lost on Scott: "Even though I was two years younger than Mike, he always found time for me, and for my family. We had a lot in common, and he was the type of guy who had everything together. He knew who he was, and I respected that about him."

FOUR

Garden Grove, California,
1997

I t was a bright afternoon in early fall; the air smelled of freshly cut and watered grass. Newly painted white yard lines sharply contrasted the green of the football field as the two teams scrimmaged. George sat quietly outside the fence watching as Michael and his teammates of the Argonaut football team went three and out again. George could see how much these young men tried to get the ball down the field, but they stood no chance against the bigger, faster, and more seasoned football players. They couldn't get a first down to move the ball into their opponent's territory or even throw a pass without it being swatted away or intercepted by the opposing defense. Michael's team was getting pummeled by their counterpart junior varsity team, which included some of the varsity players.

One by one, the JV players on his team began to remove their helmets and quit, walking off the field in defeat and shame. They were not willing to be humiliated any longer in front of their family or friends during the Garden Grove football scrimmage.

The clock sounded its loud horn for halftime, and each team jogged to their respective locker rooms. As George sat by his old '64 gold Riviera and waited for the game to resume, Michael walked past his father with barely a glance in his direction. George watched curiously as Michael moved around the front of the car and opened the passenger door to get in. George, confused as to why Michael was not headed back to the field, looked directly at him. "What happened, Mikeys? Why are you here?"

Michael looked up at his father, his whole demeanor ripe with disappointment as he fought back tears. "Dad, they just quit. The referee canceled the game because too many of our players quit. Dad, why would they quit? We still had a chance; we still could have won."

"Mikeys, you guys were down by fifty points."

"I know, Dad, but the game wasn't over yet; we still had a chance." He hung his head trying to fathom what had just transpired as he quietly repeated again to himself, "They just quit." Quitting was not something the Monsoors did; they were taught to always follow through.

Michael's lionhearted determination grew stronger as he grew older. He played as a defensive end for the

Argonaut varsity football team while he was in high school and was known for being one of the hardest workers on the field.

Asthma continued to challenge Michael, but he was not going to let it dictate how he lived. Sally remembers how the Santa Ana winds coming in from the mountains each fall would affect Michael's breathing. One afternoon she opened the door to his bedroom to find him wheezing. She asked him why he wasn't using his inhaler.

"I'm weaning myself off, Mom."

Although unable to fully rid himself of the ailment, Michael never let it stop him from accomplishing what he set out to achieve.

———

About a year after graduating, Michael enlisted in the United States Navy. Military roots ran deep in his family. His father was a marine veteran who served as a marine helicopter crew chief. Both of his brothers, James and Joseph, were marines as were numerous relatives. So when Michael told his father he wanted to enlist in the navy and attempt to become a Navy SEAL, a special operations combat division of the navy formed by President John F. Kennedy in 1962, he was immediately teased for being a black sheep among a family of marines.

As a child, Michael often asked his father all about the UDT (Underwater Demolition Team) Frogmen, the precursors to the SEALs, who cleared beaches of obstacles during World War II. These men would swim into the beach and clear paths for the marine landing craft using high explosives to complete the job. George also told Michael of the SEALs in Vietnam. Their mission was to conduct clandestine direct action operations in coastal waters and rivers. George would tell him stories about their incredible secret operations and assistance in the Vietnam War. He didn't realize then that Michael was seriously considering joining the navy to become a SEAL. Once Michael learned about the intensity of their training and the core mission of the SEALs, he was hooked. There was no other option for him in his mind. He was joining the navy and he would be a Navy SEAL.

Michael officially enlisted in the navy on March 21, 2001. He was sent to Navy Basic Training in Great Lakes, Illinois, and after graduating, he attended Quartermaster "A" School. From there, he arrived in Coronado, California, to begin his training at Basic Underwater Demolition SEAL training (BUD/S). After a few weeks of indoctrination, he joined up with BUD/S class 238 and was immediately thrust into the chaos that is First Phase. Before dawn broke on day one, Michael and his classmates were well into this new and violent process of separating the physically and mentally weak from the strong. The first day begins with the fabled "grinder PT" and continues with evolutions involving repetitions of lifting and running miles carrying a 300-plus-pound boat or a 150–200-pound log with a boat crew of six to seven men. There is not a moment without some type of physical evolution designed to test might and mettle. The days continue like this for weeks with the only reprieve arriving on Saturday and Sunday, given to students to allow recovery from the previous traumatic five days. Michael and his classmates would come to know the real meaning of "The only easy day was yesterday."

By this time, it was now late fall of 2001; the days were shorter, and the air was cooler. Michael was exhausted and decided to head home for the weekend to get some much-needed rest in the midst of his vigorous training. George knew something was wrong as soon as Michael returned home. Michael wasn't walking right, and as George looked down at his feet, he could see why. Michael's socks were bloody, and Michael was miserable.

"Michael, what are you doing? You are not going to make it like that."

"Dad, I'm not quitting."

"Michael, you can't even walk, and your feet are a bloody mess; you're leaving footprints all over the kitchen floor."

"I'm not quitting."

Michael bandaged up his wounded feet as best he could and headed back to Coronado to prepare for training the following day. The bandages did little to keep the sand out of the lesions on his feet, and every step he took was like running sandpaper across the open sores, bringing excruciating pain. Both feet were an absolute mess. Yet Michael pushed on.

The pain continued to build and was not only draining him mentally but rapidly slowed his pace, affecting his ability to perform the required evolutions. He was disgusted with what had begun to creep into his conscious thought. He hated to see weakness in others but hated it even more in himself. With every pain-filled step it became clearer, and he was forced to acknowledge what he had tried to ignore, the reality that he would not be able to continue.

It was the twenty-fourth hour of the first day of Hell Week, the third week of the six-month pipeline and regarded as the most challenging week of the BUD/S training cycle, when students are expected to run upwards of two hundred miles and are allowed only around three to four hours of sleep the entire week. Michael stood up and did what he thought he would never do. He walked over to the notorious bell affixed to a pillar directly in front of the First Phase office and rang it three times, alerting the whole compound that he was finished.

Michael looked up and could see his reflection in the small window of the office door. He saw his sandy and tattered woodland cammies that only hours before were clean and pressed; he looked at his boots that only a few days before had been gleaming with polish and were now dull and cracked. Finally, he viewed the reflection of his helmet, the pride of a BUD/S student at the time as they were required to have them inspection ready for Monday morning, which meant hours of sanding and applying a final coat of dark green paint, the color of First Phase.

Devastated, he glanced at the numbers affixed to either side of his helmet . . . 238 . . . his class number, knowing that they would continue on without him. Michael made a left face and walked achingly down the sidewalk that was already lined with the helmets of those who had not made it to this point. When he reached the end, he made one more left face, took off his helmet, placed it next to the others, and quit.

FIVE

The heavy steel radiated with heat and cast precarious shadows in the bright sunlight, having just been welded together not long before this cool, spring morning in May. There was an entire force of workers in the shipyard behind the module that had been brought out on a transit system, the module weighing four thousand tons by itself. It was the foremost piece of all of the major blocks that would come together before completing this titanic endeavor. Around a thousand spectators had gathered this morning. The air was brisk, but the morning was beautiful in Bath, Maine, at Bath Iron Works, a ship manufacturing company. In business since 1884, Bath Iron Works has created, built, and supplied naval warships in defense of the United States for over a century and throughout both world wars. The workforce today is made up of employees from every type of background with all different skills who come together to create the latest and greatest warships the world has ever seen.

Today was a special day at Bath Iron Works made even more so because of how unique this monstrous task had been for the company. Today, the thousand or so workers and spectators would witness a tradition known as the keel-laying ceremony. In the past, this is when the backbone of the ship was laid as the first foundational block to start the building of the rest of the ship. In modern ships, this is done in sections called modules that are placed, fitted, and tack welded to ensure specifications are met. In the end, this event signifies the beginning of assembly that, in this case, was years in the making, with more to go. This ship was to be one of the most innovative designs as well as one of the largest ships the company had ever created.

Made in a group of three, the DDG-1000–class guided-missile destroyers were created specifically to combat emerging threats worldwide. These three ships are grouped into a class bearing the name of Admiral Elmo Zumwalt, the youngest ever appointed chief of naval operations, who served through World War II and the conflicts of Korea and Vietnam, until 1974. When he became CNO at age forty-nine in 1970, he led sweeping reforms, including the modernization of numerous frigates and fighter jets that drastically improved the efficiency and fighting capability of the US Navy as well as humanizing the naval enterprise. He became famous for his messages to the fleet, known as Z-grams, which he sent out as directives to his subordinates on matters that covered all subjects of service from haircuts to the equality of minorities and women serving in the navy.[1] His belief was that the person and performance was more important than procedural doctrine. He left behind a legacy that still rings on today. The first of the DDG-1000 Zumwalt-class warships is named the USS *Zumwalt*, hull number 1000; the third will be named the USS *Lyndon B. Johnson*, hull number 1002. This ship undergoing construction is the second.

The stealthy, powerful, and lethal design of this warship will span current needs to future capabilities. All three of the warships were designed to combat the threats of today as well as those in the coming decades by adding space and power that can accommodate warfighting systems and capabilities not yet imagined. Each of the ships is equipped with numerous advance technologies and survivability systems.[2] The architecture of the class produces a low radar signature that makes them less noticeable when sailing the high seas. The designers achieved that by working directly with the navy and included specific items, such as creating angles that redirect radar energy and giving the bow a forward sweep, which allows the ship to cut through the water causing far less wake. The ship is colossal: the overall length is 610 feet, about two football fields, and the weight is a staggering sixteen thousand tons.

The entire power system created for the ship uses state-of-the-art technology that allows, if one section is hit in battle, for continued operation in other sections. Most ships Bath Iron Works had created up until this series used a unique power system for each division of the ship. The entire shipbuilding process takes about six years to complete, and this DDG-1000 series was pushing the boundaries with the latest and greatest modernization.

Men and women from different backgrounds and skills have dedicated their entire careers to creating these ships, and it is not uncommon to celebrate numerous forty-year employees each year. A testament to loyalty and pride of their craft was exemplified by the workers, and that was not lost on the two honored guests who were with them on this special day, May 23, 2013. Today was quite different than the others for the Bath Iron Works employees; on this day, they were taking a moment to stop their intense physical work, their designing, welding, and engineering, to witness the event unfolding before them. They watched intently in silence as the two visitors, who were covered in welding gear from head to toe, walked slowly over to the massive steel module housing the keel unit. The silence was broken by the sound of an electric arc hitting the heavy steel plate. Sparks shot in all directions from the blinding point of light as the two guests took turns welding each of their initials into the keel plate of the ship.

The keel-laying is the first of three ceremonies in the life of a new ship, symbolizing the ship's transition from a mere concept to a product that will one day become a US warship.[3] Navy tradition has celebrated this special keel-laying ceremony for hundreds of years.

As the two guests continued welding their initials into the steel module in honor of the ship's namesake, the shipbuilders and spectators looked on. They had seen this done many times before, but this time was unique. Their ships had been dedicated to all types of important figures, each special in their own way, but there was an aura about the two individuals that emitted quiet strength and humility; it made the workers proud. Proud of the work of their hands and the honor it bestowed, for their country and fellow men and women. As each initial was melted into the keel plate, silence yet again gripped the scene for just a few moments, but it was necessary, an act of respect that each employee wanted to give. It was the least they could do for the visitors at hand. Then, as quickly as the work stopped, it began again. The loud sounds of steel being pounded, shaped, welded, and forged together resumed in unison with the heavy clanking of tools and machinery as they continued to build the DDG-1000–series ship piece by piece. This warship, the second in the series of three, would bear the hull number 1001.

SIX

Sicily, Italy,
2002

Mike took a few steps forward, drew a deep breath, and jumped. For a moment he felt weightless as the drop caused his heart to jump into his throat. The face of the giant, jagged rock blurred by. Mike plunged into the refreshing, clear water below. One moment surrounded by open air and the next, the beautiful marine life of the Mediterranean. One by one, his friends joined him.

They called themselves the "Aci boys," named for Aci Trezza, the small, picturesque city in Sicily, Italy, where they were currently stationed at the naval air station in Sigonella. Chris, Mike, Ali, and their buddy Salem had recently completed a course that trained them to become auxiliary police officers and were given a two-year billet that tasked them with providing base defense. For most of these men, however, it was the surest and fastest way to get back to BUD/S for a second chance to realize the lofty goal of becoming a Navy SEAL.

They were on top of the tallest of five basaltic rock formations that jutted from the bright Sea of Sicily right in the center of the Mediterranean. Their surroundings were something postcards were made of: the crisp, blue sky overlooking the crystal-clear waters attracted visitors from all over the world because of Aci Trezza's breathtaking landscapes. The town is most famous for the *faraglioni*, which are three sea stacks and five rocks jutting skyward from the sea having been shaped by thousands of years of erosion from wind and water.

What makes the faraglioni fascinating is their association with the legend of Odysseus. The legend says that on his journey home from the Trojan War, Odysseus made landfall on the Island of the Cyclops, where he was "greeted" by the savage, man-eating giant Polyphemus. The cyclops devoured many of Odysseus's travel companions. To escape, Odysseus devised a plan to make Polyphemus drunk, then blinded him. Enraged, Polyphemus began to throw large boulders at Odysseus's ships as they were sailing away, thus giving rise to the faraglioni formation.

These rock formations are now known to the locals as "Islands of the Cyclops," because, according to the legend, the cyclops—in Greek and Roman mythology, members of a primordial race of giants with a single eye in the center of their foreheads—once had a smithy below Mount Etna, which looms over Aci Trezza to the northwest.[1]

This collection of five jagged, basalt rocks stood at all different heights, but Michael and his friends only cared about the tallest one, which Chis Holuka endearingly called the "L'der rock" because it seemed to be somewhat in the shape of an *L* and loomed around sixty-five feet above the sea. Michael and his buddies not only enjoyed the thrill of jumping off of that rock, but used it as a natural tool to prepare themselves to return to BUD/S. Increasing the strength and endurance of mind and body was the main goal, and as each of them plunged into the invigorating water, they'd dive as far down as their lungs would allow, sixty to seventy feet below.

Over time, they could dive down farther and farther, viewing all kinds of exotic sea life, from octopi to jelly-fish to capone, more commonly known as mahi-mahi or dolphinfish. When they absolutely needed to take a breath, they would surface and began all over again: climb up the towering rock careful to avoid all of the sea urchins that had affixed themselves along its sides at the ocean's surface, free-fall back down into the water, dive as far as they could, and swim back up for air. Each year there was a mother sea gull, a *gabbiano* in Italian, who guarded her baby gulls and would attack anyone or any-thing that came near the nest. Ali Atash-Sobh recalls with laughter how they had to wait until her young had hatched or it was bad news for all of them. "We'd climb that rock almost every day in the summer and the free fall was the most exciting part. We'd fall to earth, plunge into the water, dive deep, then resurface gasping for breath. We did it so often, my back started to ache from the continual compression of hitting the water."

What some would think of as a crazy or thrill-seeking stunt was just another day for Michael and his friends, who were determined to push themselves as hard as necessary to train their bodies for the rigors of BUD/S. They were getting a second shot and they were not about to blow it. They would do whatever it took to be ready this time around. Michael's most traumatic experience thus far in his life was ringing the bell and quitting BUD/S, and he would not be satisfied without a second chance to prove to himself that he could do it. He told his younger brother, Joe, that this second time around, they would have to drag his dead body off the beach before he would quit.

———

Nightlife abounded in Sicily, and there was no shortage of areas to explore. Michael's love of cars and adventure still rang through, and he couldn't be prouder of the vehicles he purchased while in Italy. Chris recalls when Michael bought a Russian truck called a Lada Niva with a manual transmission. He loved to race it down Mount Etna, a massive mountain near where they lived in Sicily. He also enjoyed taking it off-roading in the neighboring town called Motta Sant'Anastasia. One late evening, Michael had his brother Joe and Ali along for the ride.

Ali remembers sitting in the back thinking, "This is a bad idea . . ." but he went along for the adventure anyway. The course was extremely dangerous, and it was pitch black outside. Michael was in his element and couldn't wait to drive through it. He flipped his floodlights on, revved the engine, and off they went. Up and down, through the ruts and uneven rocks and finally after what felt like an eternity, he slammed on the breaks and let out a gregarious laugh. "Guys, look, we almost died!" Ali wasn't sure if he was joking or serious, but then he looked outside of the truck just forward of where they had come to an abrupt stop, and there they were, on the edge of a rocky, steep cliff. Michael had managed to make it through that night and many more unscathed, but not all of his vehicles did.

Michael also purchased a Lancia, an incredibly fast car with all-wheel drive, and used it to cruise all throughout Italy, the higher the speed, the better—until one afternoon when Ali got a call from Mike. He had crashed it racing an Audi on the *autostrada*. They were flying down the Sicily highway when Mike hit a wet spot and lost control. His Lancia spun and slammed directly into the concrete divider wall. Luckily, he wasn't hurt and was able to get it towed back to his home, but it was not looking good for the car. Ali drove over to Mike's apartment to see how he could help. First, he saw the car; it was totaled. Then, he saw Mike, a beer in his hand, a steak on the grill, and not a care in the world. "It was good while it lasted," Mike said, with his signature smile.

He was never one to hold back. He convinced Chris to jump his own rental car over a washed-up section of road that unintentionally formed a skateboard-like ramp, and Chris went for it. There they flew, with all four wheels off of the ground, and it was glorious. Two guys having a blast, pushing the car to its max and seeing if it could perform. It absolutely did, but Mike got into so many accidents in Italy, he opted to pay two hundred dollars a day extra for car rental insurance just to cover his shenanigans, because he had no intention of letting up.

The time spent in Sicily brought about something that can never be replaced in the "Aci Trezza" boys' minds: memories of their time with Mike when they grew as men and fostered lasting friendships. They pushed themselves and each other and dug deep into meaningful discussions on matters of importance, such as religion and duty to their country. Mike was a goofy, fun-loving guy willing to snowboard in the southern Italian mountains who once substituted his high-top tennis shoes in place of snowboarding boots. At the same time, he stood quietly for his convictions of faith and demanded respect from those around him, often by communicating with only his eyes. Chris remembers Mike not speaking to him for a few weeks when Chris made a smart aleck remark and sped away from Mike in his car. When Chris finally came around to apologizing for his less than admirable behavior, Mike bluntly replied, "Dude, sometimes you're too loud and you talk too much." Chris remembered that experience vividly because it was such a strong example of Mike's determination not to be disrespected for being who he was, which meant calling out friends in their mistakes if need be.

Ali and Chris recall how deeply Mike loved his country and missed being away from the US while stationed in Italy. Even amid the excitement and adventure of exploring all of Europe together, Mike still found time to host BBQs at his apartment—with a grill Chris had painted and coined "Big Mike's grill"—every Sunday that followed a long weekend off from their base patrol. Grilling, he told them, was an American pastime, and he wanted to create that experience right where they were in Aci Trezza. Mike would mix up his own marinades, one for chicken and one for steak, and stock his fridge with the foods he knew his friends especially enjoyed. He was always putting his friends first, and it was there that the young men relaxed and rejuvenated for the coming week ahead. They'd often watch a quintessential American movie like *Dazed and Confused* or *Escape from New York*.

As the two years came to an end and he inched closer to heading back to Coronado for his second shot at BUD/S, Michael felt strong and ready. He still contended with his severe asthma, which caused him to rarely be without an inhaler while working out, but he would not concede to this ailment in any shape or form. One afternoon as Chris and Mike ran side by side on one of their last hard runs, Mike pushed himself harder and harder to beat his time and his friend. As Chris pulled ahead, a pissed-off Mike grabbed his inhaler, chucked it across the road, and sprinted until he beat Chris and finished the run. That was the last time Chris ever saw Mike use his inhaler. He didn't have room for weakness; it was all or nothing this time around.

SEVEN

"Three, two, one . . . Bust 'em." The First Phase instructor spoke quietly through his megaphone. The resounding effect produced an eerie feel to the already ominous environment.

The pungent scent was thick, the air smelled of urine and sweat intertwined with ocean saltwater and seaweed. Michael and his crew were sprinting so closely to each other that even one misstep would cause the entire boat crew to tumble to the sand. The inflatable boats thrust together violently as the students struggled to stay on their feet and outpace their opponents. Feet slipped on the steep, downward slope to the left, and bodies crashed into the sandy berm to the right; either side was just as precarious, and one wrong move would result in defeat.

It was "Hell Week." The evolution was called Drag Races and was often done just after coming back from chow. With boats on their heads, the two boat crews would line up on a narrow strip of beach with a steep drainage ditch along one side and a tall sand berm on the other. The winning crew was rewarded with some kind of short physical reprieve or type of sweet snack. There were no rules, just win. It was not uncommon for one or both crews, boat and all, to end up in the ditch or up onto the berm.

A boat crew is made up of six to seven students matched by height. Their Inflatable Boat–Small (IBS) weighs 350 pounds without the wooden paddles, sand, or water in them, which often added fifty to a hundred extra pounds. Moving it from one place to another was a challenge and needed to be done in unison as the students walked, ran, or carried the boats on their head or in their hands, all the while exhausted, soaking wet, sandy, and cold. During Hell Week a crew rarely went anywhere without their boat; it was part of them.

Only a few weeks prior, what would be BUD/S class 250 was beginning indoctrination—a first time for many of the young men who were ready and willing to jump into this intense training to see if they had what it took to become a US Navy SEAL. For Michael, it represented a second chance, and he was determined to succeed. He'd been training and patiently waiting for two years for this opportunity and was not going to let it slip away.

There Michael sat, in his "dunga jams," a nickname for the working uniform of the fleet navy at the time. The nickname was a holdover from the old dungaree working uniform. It was not too dissimilar with the same light blue top but instead had dark blue cotton bottoms in place of the dungaree trousers. This would be one of the last times Michael wore this uniform. He would soon transition into a new uniform, woodland camouflage, that was worn only by Navy Seabees and Naval Special Warfare personnel. As Michael remained seated, filling out his medical paperwork outside the BUD/S medical building in preparation to begin training, Michael's classmate Gabe Lynch recalls running into him for the first time. "He was a guy who was gregarious and always cracking jokes. I instantly could tell he had this coolness about him." Gabe was a farm boy from Oregon, and Mike, a Southern California city boy; they seemed an unlikely pair, but that day was the beginning of a close friendship that would involve all kinds of adventures together. Both were excited, and each day was a day closer to their end goal of becoming a Navy SEAL and deploying in service to their country, something they could not wait to do.

The Naval Special Warfare's (NSW's) mission post-Vietnam had primarily been Foreign Internal Defense. It involved training allied and friendly military units around the world in how to conduct special operations. But as soon as Islamic terrorists attacked on September 11, all of that changed. The president and

Congress broke the proverbial glass, and NSW was called upon to put into action what they were trained to do. They willingly accepted the task and went to war.

Every one of the BUD/S students in class 250 remembered exactly where they were when those terrorists used passenger aircraft to kill thousands of Americans. Many recall feeling intense anger for those who carried out the plot, others felt empathy for the Americans who lost their lives, but almost all BUD/S students shared a common reaction the morning of 9/11: a deep sense of duty. They were young, strong, and athletic men who could have chosen to do anything they wanted with the opportunities available to them. They chose to not seek fulfillment elsewhere and live according to their every whim and desire but instead to seek something much more deliberate and life-changing. They chose to forego those opportunities for the time being in exchange for seeking recompense and justice, to nullify an existential threat to their country and fellow men and women, and ultimately the American Dream. They could not wait to get their chance to respond to the aggressors who chose to attack their fellow countrymen and women.

Gabe and Michael were both a part of Boat Crew 3. They were close in height, standing just around six foot one. Gabe recalls how Mike was always one to brighten the mood of the guys during the often exhausting days of being beaten by the ocean surf while wet and sandy all day long. One by one, guys began to quit, and eventually Gabe was shifted to Boat Crew 2. Mike lamented,

"Man, they are breaking up the all-star crew!" It didn't take long for even more men to quit, and Gabe was shifted back to Boat Crew 3 with Mike.

Gabe was the slower runner between the two of them, and he remembers Mike hanging out in the back with him as they would push through their four-mile timed runs. He would encourage Gabe, then sprint back up to the front and finish easily in the top tier of runners every time. That was the kind of guy Mike was, always looking out for his buddies. He could see who needed a word of encouragement or action of support and would deliver it at just the right time. Sometimes, that's all it took when a guy was delirious, running on a few hours of sleep for days on end.

Multiple BUD/S students recall being at their darkest moments and experiencing very different outcomes. For one guy, when he voiced his struggle and questioned any reason to continue through the rigorous training, not one other crewmate encouraged him to keep going. That is what did it for him. He felt, in that dark moment, that although he sought the SEAL brotherhood, the brotherhood did not want him. He thought to himself if that is the case, why continue? He rang the bell and laid down his helmet in defeat.

Another SEAL recalls also experiencing a dismal moment in the thick of Hell Week when he, too, questioned his reasons for staying and if it was actually worth the suffering they were going through. It took only one crewmate speaking a few words to knock him out of his own mental struggle: "Shut the fuck up, and keep going." That one phrase, one man caring about his fellow man, is all it took. He never thought again of quitting and felt the accomplishment of finishing training a few months later. Michael had moments like those when he was there for Gabe and numerous other good friends in more ways than one. Even though Michael had not made it yet and become a part of the SEAL brotherhood, brotherhood itself was something he already understood in the depths of his core. He was not going to let his friends down.

It was now the second to last day of Hell Week, and Gabe and Mike had just finished doing dying cockroaches: lying flat on their backs and holding up their feet and arms for what felt like eternity. At this point, the guys had been up for almost four days with around three to four hours of sleep total. Gabe remembers each of them fighting mentally to stay awake and how hard they all struggled against dozing off, although many of them had their moment when they succumbed and began to close their eyes. If that happened, someone would jam an elbow into the guy or shake him to make sure he stayed awake.

Gabe was holding out fairly well at that point, but staying alert was getting tougher and tougher. It was time to move, and they lifted the boats that, at this point, felt like lead weights in their tired and sore arms. They marched collectively into the bay. The water was cold, and their boots sank deeply into the silty bottom.

On the opposite shore, the San Diego lights were bright against the dark evening sky, and their reflection on the bay lit up the scene. Under different circumstances, the men may have stopped to appreciate the picturesque view. The light, however, brought no solace, only aiding in illuminating the daunting task ahead. At about waist deep, each of the men first straddled and then sorely climbed into the boats; they knew that this was the home stretch. With paddles in hand they began to row in unison. They had just taken the first few strokes in an evolution aptly named "Around the World," which entailed paddling their small boats from the San Diego Bay north through the channel around the tip of Coronado Island and then back south to BUD/S beach, a staggering thirteen miles. As they paddled, Gabe couldn't hold back any longer; he started to doze off, and without missing a beat, Michael shouted over to him from his side of the boat, "Hey, man, I love you, bro, but you need to wake up!"

That's all it took to jar Gabe back to consciousness and help him focus. It had taken all night, and as the sun rose, Michael and Gabe could see the BUD/S beach. Their boat was leading the group but was only barely in front of the "smurf" crew. This is the name awarded to the boat crew that is made up of the shortest members of the BUD/S class. They often lose many foot races, but this was no foot race, and as always, it paid to be a winner. Both crews began to paddle hard to be the first to the beach. As they entered the surf zone, Michael's crew was in the lead. All they had to do was catch a wave and ride it into the shore. Easier said than done. Whether coming in or going out, traversing the surf zone is no insignificant feat to accomplish with an IBS. First, a crew must pick the perfect time during the wave set. Then, they must work in unison to speed up or slow down the boat to keep it in the trough between the waves before they begin to break. A crew can then choose to ride in behind a breaking wave or in front. Whichever position is chosen, the goal is to stay away from the plunge and keep the boat straight at all times. Even small waves are capable of folding an IBS in half, affectionately called "getting taco'd," and if the coxswain cannot keep the boat straight, the waves can capsize it, sending the crew head over heels into the ocean.

Michael's boat entered the surf perfectly; they paddled hard as the trailing wave began to build. They were on pace to win, but as the boat picked up speed, a last-second decision by the coxswain caused the IBS to turn hard broadside to the cresting wave. There was no saving it: the wave curled, standing the boat up vertically on its side. Then it crashed, slamming boat and crew upside down into the freezing water. The men surfaced only to see the "smurf" crew safely landing their boat on the beach and finishing first. There would be no winner's reward for Michael's crew.

It was Friday morning, and in only a few hours, class 250 would secure Hell Week having lost about 75 percent of their original number. This time, Michael remained.

Once through Hell Week, the next few weeks of First Phase passed smoothly for Michael. Class 250 began Second Phase, where the focus is open- and closed-circuit combat diving. The students start with open circuit, learning dive physics along with practical application in a large pool called the Combat Training Tank.

The series culminates in a dive known as Open Circuit Eight or the Pool Competency Test. One of the last major tests consists of the instructor progressively inducing malfunctions that require students to follow a specific procedure in sequence to find and fix the issue. The test begins with a simulated surf hit, a violent assault from the testing instructor where the student is tossed and tumbled along the bottom of the pool while having his mask and mouthpiece ripped away. This goes on for anywhere from fifteen to thirty seconds. After the hit, the student comes to rest only to find that his mask is nowhere to be found and his air source is no longer working. It is at this point when he will begin the procedure to fix his equipment and reestablish his air source. This cycle continues for twenty minutes as the problems become more dire and more complex culminating in a malfunction that is unfixable. The student is still required to get through as much of the procedure as possible. If he can no longer continue and still does not have a working air source, he gives the testing instructor a hand signal asking to perform a Free Swimming Ascent (FSA). The instructor gives consent with two taps to the student's head and guides him to the surface. When at the surface, the student is critiqued on his performance and told if he is a pass or fail. This test is designed to induce hypoxia and stress to evaluate the student's ability to manage panic and involuntary muscle response, abilities vital to combat performance.

Rey Baviera, another friend of Michael's who became the lead petty officer (LPO) of their BUD/S class during Second Phase, recalls how he would have rather passed out in the water than bolt to the surface. "Time moved slowly in the water, and our brains were working on overdrive; there is a specific sound like a deep, muffled gulp you make when you are consciously fighting your physiological response to breath, which gets even more rapid the longer you hold your breath. You have to fight your natural instincts. And the tread . . . oh, the tread was dread. You are wearing your gear plus dive weights and fins, and you have to tread water for five minutes while keeping your hands at the wrist level out of the water. If your hands go below the water, you fail. It was miserable!"

———

Michael was no stranger to the water and completed Second Phase without issue. But before Michael and his friends moved onto the third and final phase, he had a little trip up his sleeve.

EIGHT

It was a short two-hour ferry ride across this stretch of the Pacific Ocean; the sun was shining brightly, and they could feel the cool sea spray on their faces. The deep blue color and clarity of the water only added to the excitement and anticipation of the three guys leaning against the rail. Directly off the coast from Long Beach, California, stood Catalina Island, a tourist island known for its abundant sea life. The weekend brought a much-needed reprieve and a nice change of scenery that for the time being helped the guys forget about the daily grind of BUD/S. Michael, being an avid adventurer, had planned a spearfishing trip and brought Gabe and another buddy of theirs, Chris Kimbrell, from their BUD/S class, along for the weekend.

Gabe knew how to spearfish like Mike, and they were naturals in the water, but for Chris, a Midwest land-locked boy, this escapade was not his forte. He was ready to go for it, though, and couldn't wait to see what the picturesque island had to offer. When they arrived, Mike had a boat rented and ready for them. They loaded up their gear, fired up the motor, and headed out into the crisp, clear water. The coast of Catalina was full of marine life: calicos, bonitos, lobster, halibut, and leopard sharks all swam off the shores. As the launch guide sent them off, he advised them they could go no farther than the eight-mile marker he pointed out. "Okay, boys, let's go; we are going to the very end of that stretch!" Michael called out as they sped off from shore.

Once they arrived at their destination around eight miles out, Mike and Gabe began to put on their gear and prepare their guns to hunt their prey. Their equipment included spearguns, shortie wet suits, fins, masks, and weight belts.

Chris was the first one all suited up and couldn't wait to get going. Before Gabe had even dropped the anchor, Chris jumped into the water to see what he could find. Moments later, he burst through the surface proudly holding up his spear. There on the end of his six-foot-long Hawaiian sling flopped a beautiful orange fish. Chris yelled in triumph. Michael immediately dove into the water tackling Chris as he pulled the spear from his hand.

"That's a garibaldi, the state fish of California; it's super illegal to hunt it, dude!" Michael yelled at Chris.

There were other fishing boats all around, and any one of them could have seen the fish that Chris had on the end of his sling. Michael quickly snatched the fish from the tip of the spear and dove to the bottom. He found a large rock and wedged the fish underneath, guaranteeing that it would not end up back at the surface.

"After I figured out what I could and could not spear, we continued the hunt. I recall holding my breath and getting as far down as I could and then coming back up for air. I checked my dive watch, and it said something ridiculous like ten to twenty feet deep. Then Mike dives down and doesn't surface for the longest time. He comes back up and his dive watch reads sixty to seventy feet. He was incredible; he was blasting all kinds of fish. So I dive back down and see what else I can find, trying to keep up with him and Gabe.

"I had no idea what I was doing." Chris laughs as he recounts the story. "The garibaldi, that's the only fish I could catch. Mike and Gabe caught all of the real game fish that we could bring back and actually eat."

Down each went with their spear guns, fingers on the triggers and hearts beating quickly . . . it was surreal to be in the fishes' element. The key to victoriously catching the fish was to be as quiet as possible; if they moved, their prey was gone in an instant. It was stunning under the water; everything moved in slow, rhythmic motion.

Closer and closer they got to calico bass, opal eye, and perch on that particular day. Michael cast his sights on a calico bass swimming by, and off he went. Carefully and intentionally he pursued the fish. Even though it wasn't huge, it was fast, and Michael had to be careful not to spook it. He kicked his fins slowly and slid through the depths with ease. He had stalked his prey well and got just close enough to shoot, hitting the fish broadside, perfect shot. Mike felt a rush of adrenaline and he pulled his prize to the surface. It was one of many catches that day as they soaked up every minute of the Pacific Ocean's marine life.

When they finally called it toward the end of the afternoon, Chris and Mike loaded back up into the boat first. They hollered for Gabe to swim back in and started to take off their gear. Chris headed to the motor to get it started. He began to pull the pull cord and, after numerous attempts, could not get it going. He called for Gabe's expertise; once Gabe had hoisted himself back in and removed his gear, he headed to join Chris at the back of their fourteen-foot boat. Getting there was a bit of a challenge. He was avoiding all kinds of fishing and diving gear as well as the numerous fish they had caught and watching each step he was taking. He looked up as he reached the back just in time to see Chris's elbow flying right toward his face. Chris had no idea Gabe was right there and accidentally ended up elbowing Gabe right in the nose as he yanked at the pull cord.

"Ahhh, I am so sorry, buddy" gasped Chris as Gabe assured him he was okay and that it wasn't a big deal. Then, Michael looked at Gabe's face and said, "Dude, your nose is completely crooked right now; it's totally broken." Michael looked back at Chris, and they both inspected Gabe's nose closer as it began to bleed.

Mike continued on, "Let's get you fixed up. Face me, ready, man . . . one, two, three," then he used his thumbs to snap Gabe's nose back into place. "You'll be all right," Michael said as he patted Gabe on the back with his mischievous grin, completely unfazed. With Gabe's help, they were finally able to get the motor fired up, cruise back to shore, and turn in the boat.

They unloaded and cleaned all of their gear and, after laying it out to dry, headed to their hotel room to shower off and clean up. The guys later ventured out to explore the town for the evening, Gabe with his swollen nose and all, to enjoy some burgers and beer before heading back to Coronado in the morning. The third and final phase of BUD/S was about to begin.

NINE

San Clemente Island, California,
2004

The sound was deafening as the stationary base element initiated the ambush on the enemy camp below. The men behind the weapons were in awe of the sheer volume of firepower they had brought to bear. The Mk 46 and Mk 48 sang back and forth as the M4 gunners, still firing, clambered to get out of the way of the violent ejection of the spent shells. The volume never slowed as the green star cluster initiated the maneuver element and signaled the base element to shift fire. "Changing!" Michael yelled as he lifted the feed tray cover of his Mk 48. His barrel glowed a dull red as he loaded his seventh hundred-round box of ammo. The maneuver element was just about to enter the kill zone, and any minute the red star cluster would pop and signal the base element to cease fire. Michael let it rip. In one long burst, he emptied the ammo box. Michael was on the last box he had carried in and yelled to his squad, "Ammo!" Within seconds, three more boxes were sailing through the air in his direction. Just as he was about to close the feed tray on his next belt, the sky lit up with bloodred streaks. The hilltop went quiet. In the silence Michael could hear the metal pinging and ticking as it cooled; the smell of burned lubricant and hot metal filled the air, and the glow of the barrel lit the immediate area in what was otherwise a dark, moonless night.

After weeks of firearms instruction and tens of thousands of rounds, this was the first time each man was able to freely fire his weapon at his discretion without a structured drill or range safety officer over his shoulder. Still full of adrenaline, class 250 had just finished their first live-fire night training raid.

Third Phase, the last training block before graduating BUD/S, entailed instruction on SEAL weapons and tactics. Lasting around eight to ten weeks, the students cover land navigation, land warfare, ambushes and raids, patrolling, weapons handling and marksmanship, and demolition.

Michael and his classmates were on San Clemente Island, focusing specifically on raids, ambushes, and demolition. They were excited to be out on the island together away from the flagpole of WARCOM (Naval Special Warfare Command), where they were not at the mercy of their instructors or being surf-tortured on a daily basis. It was their last hooyah, and they loved it. This was the point when each man began to feel and understand the SEAL mentality on a deeper level.

San Clemente Island is a rocky, volcanic island off the coast of California with hardly any trees, lots of cactus, no natural fresh water, and full of caves and caverns formed by gas bubbles in the lava when the island was a molten mass.

As the men focused specifically on ambushes and raids, Rey Baviera, who continued as Michael's squad LPO through Third Phase, recalls how Michael would find a way to make light throughout the arduous and nonstop evolutions, bringing humor to any situation, brightening everyone's mood.

This last training block involved learning how to prepare for an operation phase by phase. The instructors would assign a target that the students needed to get to, then walk them through how to create a mission plan for an ambush. The students would designate which squad took on what role, the navigation route to the target, and then patrol there on foot during the night in full combat equipment to conduct the ambush and subsequent raid.

Rey remembers how they would wrap up their shins with pieces of foam sleeping mats and rigger's tape to provide a buffer against the prolific devil's walking stick plant. Ready and with game faces on, class 250 moved quickly and quietly through the rocks and foliage in full gear head to toe. They were getting their first taste of what the men had joined to do. It was a live-fire exercise;

the instructors were on-site and guided the men but still allowed the students to call the shots. The class divided into two equal groups, a base element and a maneuver element. As class 250 approached the objective, the base element took the lead and moved to establish their firing position. The maneuver element then broke off and continued to their preplanned position. The two groups formed an L-ambush around the target. Once set, the elements used radios to communicate that they were in position and ready to engage the target. The quiet night erupted with the sound of automatic weapons and M4 rifles.

"Our base element initiated the contact first, which signaled to everyone to engage the target simultaneously," Rey recalls of the engagement. "After a couple of minutes of an intense round of fire on the target site, a call was made to cease fire. After there was complete silence, another call was made to shift fire, which instructed the base element to point their weapons a few degrees off the target site and away from the maneuver element direction so that the maneuver element could approach and clear the target. A few short seconds after, the maneuver element crested the terrain they were using as cover. Walking shoulder to shoulder, they continued to fire and move through the target."

When the target was clear and the mission completed, class 250 patrolled away leaving as quietly as they had arrived.

Although the procedure was the same, each ambush and raid was unique with different sets of problems to solve.

"One of the mornings following a long night, we were all dead tired and left our gear and equipment dirty and in disarray with the intention of picking it up after getting a few hours of sleep," Rey reminisced. "The instructors took note and without warning let us have it: in addition to iterations of hitting the surf and buddy carrying, we would all be sleeping outside on the beach the following night as punishment."

It was a cold night with a strong sea breeze coming off the ocean, and the only piece of gear the men were allowed was a simple sleeping bag. The instructors took it one step further and would not allow any of them to secure their weapons in the armory. In turn, all of the students were left sleeping with their guns. If the instructors were able to take their rifle from any of them or if it was left alone, it was a huge safety violation and could get a guy sent home and possibly dropped from training. Even though they were all getting punished and it was miserable in the moment, Rey said what an awesome time it was for all of them. It built great memories and solidified their connection as brothers.

Third Phase was coming to a close just a few weeks later, and as the men prepared to graduate, they were discussing what gift to give to the command in their memory. They all wanted to leave something in their name from BUD/S class 250 that was immovable and unique. They decided to give the Basic Training Command an enormous boulder with their names engraved upon it. Now the class had to figure out how to track down a boulder, engrave it, and have it delivered to the command. Rey's wife, Maria, was back home in San Diego and took care of the logistics. What began as an idea quickly escalated into a four-ton boulder that would have to be delivered by a crane and would end up costing $7,000 and change. Each guy was given the option to back out after the final pricing was determined, and not one guy did; they were all in this together.

What the final gift became was something none of the BUD/S students would forget. And their memory forever lives on etched into the boulder that was engraved with the following words: "The actions of the few dictate the fate of many" by Alexander the Great and "The secret to BUD/S is under this rock."

History confirms the former phrase exemplified by a handful of heroes from generation after generation. The latter phrase is an ode to challenge each reader, as there is no true secret to be found by the senses. The secret lies within those who have the mental and physical fortitude to reach deep within and tear it from under the hesitation and memories of all those who scoffed and doubted, within those who find comfort in bearing pain with patience, who, in the end, will submit to defeat only if dead or too broken to continue. This is where the secret lies and they must find it within. Each student often reminded themselves in their own individual way. Fittingly, Michael wrote on the bottom of his BDU cover, the hat he wore or carried with him daily, "Don't ever quit."

As the men prepared to leave San Clemente and become Navy SEALs, they took a moment to enjoy their final night outside in the quiet air and cool breeze of their compound with a campfire on the beach at BUD/S Cove. And it wasn't just any normal campfire; they took it upon themselves to feed it plenty of wood to last all night, including all of the outside furniture: wooden benches, chairs, and even a picnic table.

It was a night to remember as they celebrated the feat they had all completed. The class had begun with around two hundred hopefuls and was now down to forty-five men who would graduate. There were thirty-four originals, including Michael, ten rollbacks, and one Egyptian national, and all had just finished arguably the most difficult training in the US military.

Michael graduated BUD/S on September 2, 2004, back on Coronado Island, California. The graduation day was memorable for all: the men stood proudly in their clean, crisp dress uniforms, and each waited with anticipation for their name to be called. Across the compound, a giant crane labored with a four-ton boulder, carefully placing the large rock in the much-deliberated position where its weight would not crush the buried utilities below it. Michael's parents, George and Sally, as well as his three siblings, Jim, Sara, and Joe, were in attendance to celebrate his achievement. George recalls the smile on Michael's face as he walked up to embrace him following the ceremony. "He had this look in his eyes that seemed to say to me, 'Dad, I hope you didn't doubt me. I told you I was going to do this, and I did it. I told you so.' I loved seeing him like that; it gave me so much joy. I never wanted him to join the SEALs, but I was so proud to be proved wrong by my son."

Following BUD/S graduation, the students headed to Fort Benning, Georgia, to complete the Army Airborne Course and then on to SEAL Qualification Training, which lasted six months and took them all throughout the United States.

Michael was pinned as a US Navy SEAL in March 2005, joining the elite force that he first heard about as a young boy when his father told him stories about the men with green faces.

TEN

The bright lights cut into the darkness as the skeleton crew of the night shift calculated their next move. Snow began to slowly fall upon the building crew, yet with perfect precision they carefully maneuvered each component into position so the nine hundred–ton composite deckhouse of the Zumwalt-class naval warship could be joined to its hull. It was a daunting and dangerous task requiring three crane operators to hoist the deckhouse in unison ninety to a hundred feet into the air and hold it steady while the ship's hull was slowly moved on a bed of wheels into position below.

It was 4:00 a.m. when the crane operator noticed the dark figure standing just outside of the brightly lit area. The snow had begun to fall more rapidly, forcing the man to squint to get a better look at who had so intently and quietly been watching the crane's every move. It took a moment, then the operator's eyes lit up with recognition. Captain Scott Smith, who was to be the inaugural commanding officer of the brand-new warship, wanted to observe in person this highly integral connection. He watched in awe as these two enormous pieces of his ship came together, literally before his eyes. It was the heart of winter, and although biting cold outside, he didn't seem to mind the elements as he witnessed history in the making.

He stood in silence. As he continued to watch, he heard a crane operator yell down to him, "Do you want to come up and join me?"

Captain Smith looked up. It was over six stories to reach the operator. "I was not thrilled, knowing I had to climb the exterior of the structure in the snow, but I felt like I needed to honor the operator and what he and the workforce do every single day, so I began to climb," Captain Smith recalled.

The operator continued to focus on the job at hand and maneuver the deckhouse into position. Captain Smith carefully climbed the sixty-five feet into the cab of the crane, and once he arrived, sat down next to the operator.

"Don't touch any buttons, sir," the operator instructed half-jokingly but completely seriously.

———

It took until almost eight the following morning for the task to be completed. The eighty to ninety workers could all breathe a huge sigh of relief, their mission accomplished. It was a success, DDG-1001 now had a secured deckhouse, which encompasses the bridge, radars, computer processing equipment, and captain's quarters along with other essential compartments.

It was one of many major feats completed as the shipbuilders continued to join together and perfect the ship. Captain Smith, however, was only beginning his forthcoming tasks as the ship inched closer and closer to full completion and welcoming her entire crew.

Each naval warship has its own crest and motto, and Captain Smith took meticulous efforts to honor the ship's namesake with each one. For the crest, he was given the parameters of simply using a shield by the Army Heraldry Command, and the rest was up to him. He knew exactly what to do in order to make sure it honored the ship and its namesake perfectly. There were a handful of people: family, teammates, and friends that he would need to talk to. He was introduced to Steve Gilmore, a retired Naval Surface Warfare captain of thirty years, who was able to connect Captain Smith with each group above and served as the nexus throughout the entire process. Captain Smith then sat down for hours with each group and learned as much as he could from them in order to create something memorable that would inspire each of his future crew members. What they collectively came up with connected the family with the navy as well as the ship's unique components.

The motto for the ship became "I Will Defend," which carries a threefold meaning: every military member takes an oath to support and defend the Constitution; another prominent military ethos states, "I will defend the defenseless"; and the Saint Michael Prayer calls upon the mighty angelic soldier to "Defend Us in Battle." Captain Smith took careful care to keep the motto in the active versus passive tense as a call to action for each sailor who serves aboard DDG-1001, and as a reminder of the ship's mission for all who learn of her.

The crest Captain Smith and his team designed showcases a prominent reinforced shield featuring a winged arm that is a heraldic representation of Saint Michael the Archangel. Behind the shield lies laurel and oak leaves—laurel for victory and oak to symbolize strength. There are also two lightning flashes on the top of the crest that represent the ship's unique propulsion. The flashes form a chevron resembling the wave-piercing bow, which is a special feature of the Zumwalt-class ships and also represents boldness. The large, inverted star above the shield is in the shape of the Medal of Honor, and it is colored purple, the traditional color of valor and sacrifice, and is inspired by the Purple Heart. The flintlock pistol represents the DDG-1001 ship's advanced gun system and, along with the Roman numeral III, is in honor of the ship's namesake.[1]

A year had passed, and after many drafts, the unique crest became finalized. Captain Smith then began to prepare for the historic naval ceremony called a mast stepping. This event has been practiced for thousands of years and traces back to the time of the ancient Romans and Greeks. When the mast was raised and connected to the ship, a coin would be placed in the exact spot that the two came together. The belief was that the coin would pay Charon, the ferryman of the underworld, to take the ship's crew across the River Styx should they perish at sea.

Captain Smith intended to make this ceremony incredibly meaningful. It was tradition for the shipbuilders to create a special box to place the coin in for the mast-stepping ceremony, but Captain Smith inquired if he and his crew could create the box instead. Bath Iron Works happily obliged. Recently, his friend and colleague Captain Sean Kerns, who was currently serving as the executive officer, had arrived from the USS *Constitution*. The USS *Constitution* ("Old Ironsides") is the oldest warship still in service in the United States Navy and was launched in 1797. It was the third of the six frigates authorized by President George Washington that made up the first US Navy. President Thomas Jefferson later used it during the Barbary Wars, and it became famous in the War of 1812 against the British Crown.[2]

Captain Smith asked Captain Kerns if he could assist in obtaining some sort of historical material from the ship, currently in the Boston Harbor. It was no small feat, but the XO was able to get Captain Smith wood from the hull of the USS *Constitution* that he and his crew used to build the box out of, honorably connecting the United States' oldest active naval warship with this newest guided-missile destroyer. He was also able to obtain pins to close and seal the box from the battleship *Missouri*, upon whose deck the Japanese Instrument of Surrender was signed in 1945.

———

It was now 2016, and the day had arrived for the contents, rich in history and heartfelt meaning, to be placed into the keepsake box by family and teammates. There were photos drawn by nieces and nephews, military coins, sand from Iwo Jima, a Saint Michael medal and prayer card, and seventeen pennies: fourteen bearing the date of 1981 and three with 2006. The dates being significant to those present.

Although the box normally would be tucked away under the mast, Captain Smith requested it to be put on full display behind thick glass in view for all who sail on or visit the ship.

With respect and reverence, the Bath Iron Works staff placed and secured the box during the ceremony. Once in place, the sponsor of the ship stepped forward, a familiar figure; it was not her first time handling a welding torch. The sparks burst from the steel, and with a steady hand, she welded it shut, sealing it indefinitely. It was a dramatic and stunning moment for all who were there to commemorate the momentous event.

The following day, June 18, 2016, the ship's christening took place. Captain Smith approached the podium of the ship to announce his crew to all attending: "Hailing from Phippsburg and the Philippines, Garden Grove and Ghana, and dozens of cities and towns in between, this crew represents the greatness of our surface navy. Each sailor has chosen to be part of the future that this ship promises, always guided by the character of the son, the brother, and the teammate who lived his life fully, with no regrets."

The captain took his seat and the ship's sponsor elegantly stepped forth to deliver a short speech about the meaning of the ship's namesake. She made such a resounding impact with her simple yet piercing words of love and gratitude that, as she finished, she was met with a crowd who rose in standing ovation and honor for her. She was then escorted to the ship's bow, her blond hair blowing lightly in the breeze. She raised a bottle of champagne into the air, and with a poignant swing, smashed it against the warship's bow proclaiming these historic words: "For the United States of America, I christen thee. . . . May God bless this ship and all who sail in her."

The crowd of a thousand spectators erupted in applause as streamers burst forth into the air. This moment marked the ship's transition from a mere hull number to a ship with a name and a spirit of her own.

DDG-1001 remained in Bath for the following two years as the systems were completed, tested, and learned by Captain Smith and his crew. The navy officially accepted the warship on April 24, 2018. Captain Smith and his crew took possession of the brand-new warship and prepared to sail her to its home port, San Diego, California.

On November 9, 2018, the ship officially set sail from the shipyard of Bath Iron Works in Bath, Maine, and into the Kennebec River. Several tugboats escorted it as it sailed down the river. It was a treacherous beginning as Captain Smith needed to focus on the task at hand, maneuvering two ninety-degree turns with the monstrous ship. He and his crew executed them with deft precision. A waving crowd hollered out cheers and farewells while they witnessed the sleek, futuristic ship glide quietly and effortlessly through the river.

Once the ship reached the mouth of the river, it passed by Fort Popham, which served as a Civil War–era coastal defense fortification. There, the crew of DDG-1001 were greeted by a final, large crowd of bystanders, who watched excitedly as it headed toward the Gulf of Maine. They had passed a major hurdle, but it was a long way to San Diego, and off the coast a storm was brewing.

ELEVEN

Michael focused and with a half-cocked smile leaned hard to the left as he took his R1 motorcycle into the sharp bend. As man and machine exited the curve, Mike opened the throttle, his bike surging beneath him. He looked to his right and saw the San Ysidro Mountains towering over the glistening Lower Otay Reservoir, which reflected the sun brightly on this quiet Saturday morning. Another curve approached, and he took it faster than the last, this time leaning hard right with his knee almost in the pavement. He added just enough counter steer to carry the speed and keep his bike from standing up and tossing him off. He checked his rearview mirror to make sure his buddy Z. was not lost behind him. Michael was going around 180 miles per hour, and Z. was working hard to stay on his tail.

Michael was not one satisfied with the average or mundane, and this bike was no exception. The Yamaha R1 is engineered for speed and stability. Even in 2005, the cutting-edge design put this bike in the top tier of motorcycles—with the best power to weight ratio of any bike at the time and frame ergonomics that made it much more rigid and stable. Michael loved the agility of the bike, and it was perfectly suited for the curvy Southern California roads he and his friends frequented in their off time.

"We bought our bikes together," said Z. "He bought a used R1 and I bought an R6, and as young guys in our twenties cruising on the weekends, we were living our best life! It was crazy trying to catch him when he'd push that kind of speed though.

"We got to know each other in BUD/S during First Phase when we were both designated to make coffee for the instructors. No one wanted to do that job because the instructors would mess with you. Mike was one to make the best of every situation, so he called me Funkmaster French Roast, and I nicknamed him DJ Decaf. We had a blast together."

Michael and Z. went through all of BUD/S together, and Z. recalls how during the land navigation portion of Third Phase, Z.'s fate ultimately came down to one final chance at passing the evolution. Land Nav is a multiday trip to Mount Laguna in the Cleveland National Forest, an hour drive from the coast of San Diego. The students are taught the basics of land navigation using a map and compass and are required to pass a practical course in the Laguna Mountains. The terrain is wooded mainly with coast live oak and pine and has rolling hills that are speckled with open glades. Many hikers and outdoorsmen love this area for those features, but class 250 was here to learn an integral war-fighting skill. The trip was rigorous, and students carried eighty- to a hundred-pound rucks during miles of hiking to navigation points. These were timed events, and, in turn, there was little time for taking a break. When not hiking, the students were learning or practicing other wilderness field craft, such as terrain association, celestial navigation tricks, and whatever else the instructors wanted to impart. In the end, the endeavor was an extremely demanding evolution and not just a stroll through the woods.

Z. managed to pass his final attempt at the course. Incredibly relieved that it was over, he entered the bus that was taking the students back to San Diego and relaxed into his seat. Just as he did so, he felt a firm grip on his shoulder. Mike sat down beside him and told him how glad he was that Z. was still there. He never forgot how genuine and caring Mike was. He had heard many others give words of encouragement while going through BUD/S, but it was always different when it came from Mike.

They both graduated BUD/S, Basic Airborne, and SEAL Qualification Training and were now assigned to SEAL Team 3, Z. to Echo Platoon and Mike to Delta. The weeks were busy training, and the weekends were spent riding their bikes, chasing girls, and hanging out with the guys. After a day of riding, they'd often come back to connect and unwind at Bar Dynamite, a small bar in Mission Bay where they'd grab drinks with friends, including Gabe and another freshly minted SEAL, Tommy D.

"Mike was living life to the fullest; he was renting this great house in Mission Bay while new guys like myself lived in small, one-bedroom apartments," said Z., laughing.

A motorcycle and a stellar pad were not the only things Michael had set his sights on. He was eyeing his next car, and he knew exactly what he wanted. He had just received a contract bonus that he used to buy a silver 2004 Corvette Z06. It had low miles, the latest tech, and it was fast, very fast.

"He was an exceptional driver, and when he'd drive us to work from the Mission Bay house we lived in together, he'd get us from Mission Bay to the Coronado Bridge in a matter of minutes, which is a twelve-mile drive. He was always up for pushing the limits and loved to drive his Corvette," Gabe remembers.

Mike was living the dream in Southern California but also understood his team was on a short fuse to surge into combat areas in the Middle East. He knew the coming months would include a firehose of information and intense training. His platoon was going to war, and how fast he learned and integrated into the platoon and his role could mean all the difference. They were preparing for a condensed work-up, normally a year and a half training cycle for each SEAL platoon, during which they travel all over the US to different training sites in preparation for the myriad of combat possibilities. Time was of the essence for the War on Terror and the enemy were hardened warfighters who cared little for the niceties and conveniences of Western culture. While Americans grew up playing video games in a culture with fractured principles, enjoying things like internet, fast food, and trophies for showing up, the enemy grew up playing with guns in a culture unified under one religion that strengthened their resolve and hardened their mettle. But the men of SEAL Team 3 Delta Platoon were hard, unified, and violent: important facets for the coming deployment in which they had only nine months to prepare.

Once Michael checked into Team 3, he became known around the command for always answering, "Roger that," anytime anything was asked of him. He said it so often, a senior leader asked what was up with the Monsoor kid who always answered, "Roger that!" In response, the leader found out that the Team 3 troop commander, Jocko Willink, had sat down the new guys and let them know that as new guys, the only appropriate response to any statement was "Roger that!" Although meant more as a way to let the new guys know what their place was, Mike made a literal go of it and became known for that precise response, happy to embrace his role as a new guy. It brought comic relief many times over as his new task unit grew to know Mike more.

One of the first blocks of their training work-up was Land Warfare out in Niland, California, located just east of the Salton Sea at the NSW Desert Training Facility, Camp Billy Machen. With a 107-degree summer average, it is a scorching place to train. This, combined with the schedule and rocky terrain scarred with washes and gullies, make it the literal and figurative crucible of work-up. Here is where the platoon will work on the tactics, techniques, and procedures of fighting in open terrain, as well as demolitions, rockets and mortars, and the different small arms weapons systems of the SEAL arsenal. A platoon is normally made up of sixteen to twenty operators each having specific roles to include snipers, breachers, communicators, and automatic weapon gunners to name a few. Although specialized within the platoon, each man is still responsible to be proficient at the other jobs. Michael and the other new guys could not wait to jump right in and get started. Michael caught on very quickly, especially with his automatic weapon, the Mk 48. Each of the new guys was being watched closely by the older men in the platoon. His LPO Doug Wallace remembers how, even though Michael was quickly picking up on the tactics and performing all tasks efficiently and without complaint, it was always with humility and a willingness to learn more. "Misery loves company, and Niland is a block where there's many reasons to complain of our intense conditions. But Mike never did once, not one time. It showed great character and understanding on his part, especially for a new guy," Doug said.

Although much of Land Warfare is spent sweaty, exhausted, and sore, it also incorporates many of the best parts of being a Navy SEAL. There are machine guns, AKs, grenades, grenade launchers, rockets, mortars, and demo. Outside of the formal instruction there is often time to have some fun to include wagers on hitting bushes with golden eggs, high-explosive 40-millimeter grenade rounds. They are golden in color and rounded at the top and often fired from an M79 or an M203 grenade launcher. Along with the standard explosive charges normally taught to and used by a SEAL platoon, experimental ones are not only allowed but encouraged with a standing competition to see who can get a certain desired effect with the least amount of explosive. Some of these include cutting railroad track or punching holes into inch-thick steel plate. Of course, just packing on the explosive will get the job done, but SEALs pride themselves on precision, and it is amazing how precise a well-designed explosive charge can be. Although a tough block of training, it is not lost on the guys that it is also a ton of fun.

Out on the West Coast there has been a long-standing practice of boxing matches within the troop. Often it is the new guys of one platoon versus new guys of the other platoon, and it was no different for Task Unit Bruiser, which was composed of the two sister platoons: Charlie and Delta.

Rey, who went through all of BUD/S with Mike, was a new guy in Delta with him and recalls, with vivid account, the look on Michael's face as they awaited what was in store for them from the older SEALs. Training was over for the day, but the day was not over. They knew whatever was going to happen wasn't going to be easy. Rey said Mike had this grin on his face that communicated to him he was not thrilled with the situation at hand. Rey wasn't sure why, then suddenly, Rey felt an arm wrap around his neck. . . .

Once Rey came to, he saw why Mike wasn't happy; Mike turned his head and Rey saw a huge chunk of hair shaved across the entire back of his head that the older guys had cut. Rey looked around and realized all of the new guys were together from Charlie and Delta Platoon and beside them lay red boxing gloves and head gear. One by one, the older enlisted SEALs paired a Charlie new guy against a Delta new guy. Each did their best to hold their own giving punch for punch, but not all fared as well as Mike. Doug recalls how Mike absolutely humbled some Charlie guys that night. Clearly, Mike knew how to fight. It came down to Mike, the last-standing new Delta guy, versus Kevin Lacz, the final remaining new Charlie guy. Kevin was huge; he was a 225-pound tower of muscle who loomed over most team guys at a height of six foot three. Mike was much smaller and more slender, but he wouldn't give up.

"He was a lean, scrappy dude," recalled Kevin. "I remember hitting him as hard as I could, but there was no shaking him. We had no boxing form; we were street fighting at that point with our boxing gloves on. I looked at him and it seemed as if his eyes were crossed as I continued to hit him over and over again, but he wouldn't stop. He returned blow after blow right back. We got so into it that I'm sure we both were seeing red, but each of us refused to back down."

Both platoons cheered and taunted as each man hit the other over and over again. Clad in only their boots and camo pants, the two men continued to brawl. Neither could defeat the other, and in the end the older men called it a tie. Kevin hugged Mike once they stopped and cooled down. "You're a tough son of a bitch, Mike," Kevin said, laughing.

Mike grinned back at Kevin, knowing that if the fight had continued, it would not have been a draw.

"Charlie platoon had these huge new guys and my guys in Delta were smaller in stature, but that night, I was so stoked with how they did, especially Mike. He solidified his place," said Dale Fortin, the Delta Platoon chief.

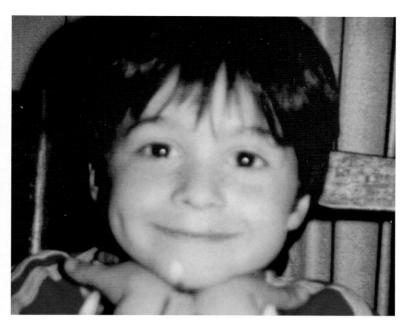

Michael at his fifth birthday party
Courtesy of the Monsoors

Michael playing hockey as a child
Courtesy of the Monsoors

Michael with his grandmother
Courtesy of the Monsoors

Chris, Mike, and Ali on their way to snowboard in Amsterdam
Courtesy of Chris Holuka and Ali Atash-Sobh

Michael by his grill
Courtesy of Chris Holuka

Boat Crew 3 after they secured Hell Week
during training at BUD/S. Gabe Lynch
on the left and Michael on the right.
Courtesy of Gabe Lynch

Michael jumping off of
"L'der rock" in Sicily
Courtesy of Ali Atash-Sobh

The Aci boys snowboarding in St. Anton, Austria
Courtesy of Chris Holuka and Ali Atash-Sobh

Michael training at BUD/S
Courtesy of US Navy

More training at BUD/S
Courtesy of US Navy

Michael and his BUD/S class 250 at their graduation
Courtesy of US Navy

George and Michael at his
BUD/S graduation
From Michael's funeral memorial pamphlet

San Clemente Island, ending
of Third Phase—packing out
Courtesy of BUD/S class 250

New BUD/S students often rub
Michael's name as they run by the
boulder out of respect for him.
Courtesy of Reynaldo Baviera

BUD/S class 250 boulder
Courtesy of Reynaldo Baviera

Michael boating during training
Courtesy of US Navy

Michael at his BUD/S graduation
Courtesy of the Monsoors

SEAL Qualification Training, Niland,
California, during the demolition
portion, where they built standard
charges (C-4) used to blow things up
Courtesy of BUD/S class 250

Michael by his Corvette
From Michael's funeral memorial pamphlet

Michael by his motorcycle
From Michael's funeral memorial pamphlet

Michael during ST-3
Delta Platoon Work-Up
*Courtesy of BUD/S ST-3
Delta Platoon mates*

Michael in Hawthorn, Nevada,
during ST-3 Task Unit
Bruiser Delta Platoon Work-Up
*Courtesy of BUD/S ST-3
Delta Platoon mates*

Michael operating during his
deployment in Ramadi, May 2006
Courtesy of Michael Fumento

Michael patrolling in Ramadi,
May 2006
Courtesy of Michael Fumento

(Left to right) Rey Baviera, Rick Nelson, Dave Garcia, and Michael in an APC conducting
a three-day overwatch of Entry Control Point 8 in the Malaab district, Ramadi, Iraq
Courtesy of Reynaldo Baviera

Michael with Rey and Smurf in Ramadi
Courtesy of BUD/S ST-3 Delta Platoon mates

More patrolling in Ramadi, 2006
Courtesy of US Navy

Michael in Ramadi
Courtesy of US Navy

In the 1st of the 506th HQ at Camp Corregidor, prepped to go on a mission
Courtesy of BUD/S ST-3 Delta Platoon mates

Michael and his Delta teammates
ready to go on one of their
final missions, September 2006
Courtesy of Doug Wallace

Michael and his Delta Platoon
mates in Ramadi, 2006
Courtesy of US Navy

Michael on Doug Wallace's
gun on September 29, 2006
Courtesy of Doug Wallace

President George W. Bush, right, walks with George and Sally Monsoor
after presenting them with the Medal of Honor on April 8, 2008.
Courtesy of US Navy and photographer Brien Aho

Sally Monsoor welding her initials into the keel plate during the
keel-laying ceremony, while the Bath Iron Works employees look on
Courtesy of General Dynamics Bath Iron Works

The USS *Michael Monsoor* keel plate, with George and Sally Monsoor's initials
welded into it, during the keel-laying ceremony in Bath, Maine, on May 23, 2013
Courtesy of General Dynamics Bath Iron Works

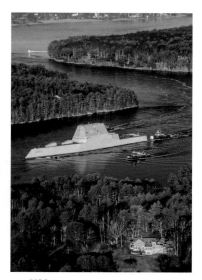

Captain Scott Smith in Bath, Maine, for the connecting of the ship, November 2014
Courtesy of Captain Scott Smith

USS *Zumwalt* negotiating the first two (90-degree) turns of the Kennebec River. You can see the tugs on each side and behind the ship.
Courtesy of Mike Nutter

Sally Monsoor holds the christening bottle alongside the ship's commanding officer, Scott Smith, her matrons of honor, and Fred Harris, president of General Dynamics, June 18, 2016.
Courtesy of Luke Lamborn

Sally Monsoor christens the future USS *Michael Monsoor* in Bath, Maine, June 18, 2016.
Courtesy of US Navy and photographer Luke Lamborn

The guided-missile destroyer *Michael Monsoor* (DDG-1001) transits the San Diego Bay.
Courtesy of US Navy and photographer Jasen Moreno-Garcia

The crew of the Navy's newest Zumwalt-class destroyer, USS *Michael Monsoor*, brings the
ship to life during its commissioning ceremony, San Diego, January 26, 2019.
Courtesy of US Navy and photographer Alex Millar

Sally with the USS *Michael Monsoor* crew when she accepted
Michael becoming an honorary chief
Courtesy of Captain Scott Smith

Doug, Benny, and Mike S. at an army memorial in
Fort Campbell, Kentucky, in Michael's honor
Courtesy of Doug Wallace

The ten-year memorial service for Michael at Fort Rosecrans Cemetery, 2016
Courtesy of US Navy and photographer Abe McNatt

TWELVE

San Diego, California,
2005

Sweat ran down Michael's face as sparks from the quickie saw burst from the rebar-reinforced door and out to his right. Just one more cut and the door would be open, allowing the first two men, referred to as the one and two man, to flow in and clear the room unimpeded. The last cut was at the top right corner of the door, and Mike had to hold the thirty-pound saw over his head and just out in front to get the right angle. In addition, he needed to stay out of the threshold of the doorway in the event that whoever may be inside decided to begin shooting through the door.

The rest of the platoon had continued to clear the structure and left Mike and the two-man entry team to finish the breach and clear this portion of it. Mike could hear gunfire in the direction of the platoon but had to stay focused. The sparks abruptly stopped, and the saw jerked into the frame as it cut through the last piece of rebar. Before Mike had even set the saw down, the one man moved to make entry. At the same moment, a burst of gunfire came through the door. The one man rolled away from the door having been hit in the shin and knee. Mike had no time to shut off the saw and dropped it. He unslung his rifle just in time to make entry, covering his other teammate who had just entered the room. Mike cleared his corner and continued to sweep his portion of the room. The enemy shooter lay against the back wall motionless, shot numerous times by Mike's teammate, the first into the room. "Clear right!" said his teammate.

Mike finished his sweep and responded, "Clear left." "Last room!" came from the right indicating that there were no more doors in the room. With that, the two men heard a voice from above. "End EX!" yelled an instructor from the rafters of the kill house, ending the exercise.

Two Troop was just finishing up at CQC (close quarters combat), a three-week training block with emphasis on clearing rooms and structures. This was one of the major blocks necessary to deploy and where Delta Platoon really began to work well as a cohesive unit.

Michael and his teammates continued to move through the different blocks of their condensed work-up still unsure of where they may be sent for their impending deployment. The SEAL teams had obligations outside of Iraq and Afghanistan that would need to be covered, and the leadership needed to decide which platoons would go where. At the end of the day, no one wanted to miss "the show," and work-up was viewed as a competition where the best platoons were picked for deployment to a combat zone.

In between CQC, MOUT (military operations in urban terrain), and the other big work-up trips, Mike and the guys still found time to squeeze in some enjoyment. Known by all of his friends for living life to the fullest, Mike would ride his motorcycle every chance he got, let his buddies drive his Corvette, and, often on weekends, head down to Calexico for a night out.

"We'd have these van wars after a night out together in Calexico or even after coming back in the evening on certain work trips," recounts Kevin Lacz. "Someone would randomly shout out, 'one, two, three, four, I declare van war!' and we'd all start brawling and trying to choke each other out. Mike was so scrappy and fast in those wars. We would go at it and our energy would last about ten minutes, and then we had nothing left. It was such a blast."

Mike managed to fit in a few more fun trips with his friends that included some unexpected excitement, which always seemed to be the standard when Mike did anything. Chris Kimbrell and Gabe remember a particular mountain-biking trip to Big Bear, California, where they took Mike's old Volvo station wagon. After an adrenaline-filled day biking down the mountain trails, they hopped back into Mike's station wagon and headed down the mountain. As the car picked up speed, Mike pressed on the brakes, but nothing happened. They began to go faster and faster down the mountain road as Mike used every driving maneuver in his toolbox to keep the car under control. While navigating the curves, he yelled to Chris who sat next to him in the passenger seat, "Oh, brakes, no brakes . . . We have no brakes!"

Chris immediately replied, "Pull the e-brake!" He hurriedly began looking for the emergency brake and found a jacket in the way. "Whose jacket is this?"

Mike shouted back, "Fuck the jacket. Pull the emergency brake!"

Mike was beginning to lose to the speed, as they approached a sharp curve with a steep drop-off. Chris pulled the brake forcefully as they were entering the turn. The car shuddered; it was just in time to decrease the momentum and make the turn. The car continued to slow as it moved down the steep hill, but now, albeit still uncomfortable, at a more manageable speed. Michael used the emergency brake to control the speed until finally coming to an area where they could release it and pull over. It was beyond intense, Chris remembers. Once stopped, they checked the brakes, which were glowing bright amber red. As the men waited for the brakes to cool, a car of people who had seen the antics coming down the mountain told them it was one of the craziest things they had seen and that their brakes looked like they were actually on fire. Just another day in the adventures of Mike.

Deployment was now only two weeks away, and the troop had just received word: they were headed to Ar Ramadi, Iraq. The men of Two Troop were ready; this was what Michael and all of his platoon mates had been training for.

In the spring of 2006, the Battle of Ramadi was just beginning, and it was already intense. "The city was inarguably the epicenter of the insurgency in Iraq and known throughout the area as 'the most dangerous city in the world,'" wrote Leif Babin, the officer in command for Task Unit Bruiser, Charlie Platoon. "The Al Qaeda leader in Iraq, Abu Musab Zarqawi, declared during that time that Ramadi would be the capital of his envisioned Islamic Caliphate in Iraq. Insurgents controlled over two-thirds of the city itself, and certain areas were nearly impenetrable to the United States and Iraqi Security Forces. US Marines and Army soldiers that were currently over there battled continually with large groups of well-armed and well-organized enemy fighters. So far, 93 US service members had been killed in action and hundreds more were wounded in nearly 15 months of fighting."

Babin continued, "The mission was clear, Lieutenant Commander Willink developed an operational strategy for Naval Special Warfare Support, which Task Unit Bruiser would follow when in Ramadi. This included aligning the SEALs with two Iraqi brigades and five US battalions. They would work directly with the Ready

First Combat Team (1 RFCT) of the First Armored Division in their strategy to 'seize, clear, hold, and build' in retaking the city. This was to be done through the establishment of Combat Outposts (COPs) constructed in previously enemy-held areas."

Michael headed north on I-5, his silver Corvette effortlessly gliding along the scenic drive that overlooked the Pacific Ocean. Time was passing quickly as he neared the departure date for his six-month-long combat deployment, and Michael was headed home to Garden Grove. As usual, he arrived home well ahead of what it would have taken the average driver. This was his final weekend to spend some quality time with his parents as well as his siblings. His family had planned a birthday celebration and going-away party. He enjoyed the evening full of food, music, and visiting with numerous relatives and friends. At one point during the party, he strolled over to his sitting grandmother with a twinkle in his eye and asked her, "Grandma, will you dance with me?"

"Well, yes, Mikey, of course!" said his grandmother, taken by surprise and breaking into a large grin.

As the up-tempo music beat in the background, Michael helped his grandmother stand and guided her back and forth, twisting, turning, and pumping their arms cheerfully to the music.

"Do you have a girlfriend, Mikey?"

"Nah, Grandma, not now. I need to focus on my work first and, plus, I'm leaving for six months."

The music ended and a new song began just as Michael performed a final overexaggerated twist and his grandmother burst into laughter. Michael was always goofing around. He continued to move through the room the rest of the evening chatting with everyone who attended the party wanting to say their goodbyes.

Early the next morning, he headed back to San Diego with his mother and sister following close behind. They agreed to help him pack up his place in Mission Bay, and there was much to be done with only one day left to do it. Michael's sister, Sara, started in his untouched bedroom, and his mother, Sally, took the kitchen. Michael worked as quickly as he could in the garage, and ultimately, they placed an entire pile of his belongings together in the center of the garage; he didn't have time to deal with them and called up one of his buddies.

"If you can help me out by grabbing a pile of my things, you can keep them all. I just need to get this place packed up so I can head out."

Michael loved nice things but was never too attached to any sort of material item and gave generously whenever he could.

Toward the end of the day, Sara headed back home early as she needed to work the next day, and Sally stayed until they finished packing and cleaning up the place. It was now close to 2:00 a.m., and Sally followed Michael outside to his silver Corvette. She opened the door and sat down in the passenger seat for the first time. She knew how much he loved his Corvette and couldn't believe she had never ridden in it until now.

"Thanks, Mom. I really appreciate your help," Michael said as he wiped the sweat off of his forehead. He then broke into a half smile. "Want to see how fast this thing goes?"

Sally smiled. "Sure, Michael. Show me."

Michael gripped the wheel and eased into the gas. Smoothly the car passed 80 . . . 90 . . . 100 miles per hour. At 120, he loosened his grip and concentrated on the feel of the car against the road. Mike smiled to himself; he couldn't believe his mom was up for the thrill ride.

At 125, Sally spoke up. "Okay, okay, that's good, Michael. Slow down!" Sally laughed and told him lovingly, "I get the point; your car can go really fast!"

They arrived back home in Garden Grove where Michael would leave his beloved Corvette during deployment. Sally bade her son goodnight and tiredly headed right to bed.

———

The time had come; George and Michael awoke early in the morning and drove back down the I-5 south to San Diego. The trip seemed to pass much faster than either would have liked. Once they arrived on Coronado, George gave his son a big, final hug as he said goodbye and a kiss on the cheek. George felt a knot deep down in his stomach, but he refused to acknowledge it. The idea that this could be the last time he saw his son was not something he wanted to think about.

As George drove home, he recalled an evening with his son from two weeks prior. He had lit up a Fuente cigar for Michael and himself on their front porch. They sat together in silence amid the cool air under the dark sky while smoke slowly drifted in the light breeze. George's voice broke the silence to address what they were both thinking: "Mikeys, what if something happens to you? It's not exactly a walk in the park over in Ramadi right now. Please don't be a hero; just do your job."

"Dad, no matter what happens, I have no regrets."

This reassurance from Mike helped, but George still did not want Mike to go. As a marine vet, George saw firsthand what war did to all of those involved, and he despised it. He knew it was unforgiving and brutal and how it could degrade and break the spirit. He also knew that Mike had been trained well by men who understood what he would be facing. This brought some consolation to George; Mike's instructors were a few of the first Navy SEALs to fight in Afghanistan and Iraq.

As they finished their cigars together that night, George looked at Mike and the man he had become. He was so proud of him; from a determined little boy who fought against the injustice of bullies and his own physical weakness of asthma, he persevered and over-came failure, adversity, and blocks of training he de-spised, such as free-fall parachuting and communications school, all with focused conviction and often a mischievous smile on his face.

———

Mike loaded up his gear and followed his teammates to the waiting C-17 aircraft. A C-17 is a multipurpose aircraft that can be configured for the transport of troops, cargo, or a combination of both. This last configuration is often how special operations units travel due to the small footprint and nature of their mission sets. TU Bruiser was no exception, and as soon as the aircraft was at cruise altitude, Michael and his friends broke out their nylon hammocks and ground pads and settled in for the long flight. The interior now looked a bit like an adult jungle gym with hammocks strung up from whatever secure spots the men could find along with sleeping bags and ground pads on the flat tops of the gear boxes. TU Bruiser had everything they needed to hit the ground running. Along with all of the team gear, each man had also packed a small box containing his personal warfighting kit that included his helmet, armor, combat uniform, boots, and all of the small accessory equipment needed for combat operations. This box is commonly known in the military as an operator's "war box." Although common equipment such as the above can be found, the rest is unique to each operator and his specific position in the troop.

Task Unit Bruiser landed at the Al Taqaddum (TQ) airport in Iraq, where they began to prepare for a short flight west to Ramadi. After the C-17 was unloaded, each operator opened his war box and donned his combat equipment. Michael had done this hundreds of times throughout work-up and his prior training trips. This time was different; this was not training, and his enemy was not other Navy SEALs trying to exploit a weakness to teach a lesson. His enemy was now hardened warfighters whose will and resolve would be used to exploit weakness in order to win the war.

Michael and his teammates gathered on the flight line and checked each other over one last time. The men were full of cautious excitement as they prepared to leave the wire into enemy territory. One by one they loaded into the Black Hawk helicopter, a UH-60 configured for combat operations. The rotors began to take the weight, and Michael could feel the machine lift off the ground. The Black Hawk cleared the surrounding buildings and date trees, and as they headed west, the men looked on at the passing villages and contemplated the possible number of insurgents awaiting them below.

"As we flew in Black Hawks toward Camp Ramadi, it began to feel real and sink in: we were headed to war," recalls Kevin Lacz.

They landed at Camp Ramadi located just west of the city across the Euphrates River. Within the walls of the camp was another compound known then as Shark Base and later Camp Marc Lee. This is where the men of Task Unit Bruiser began their deployment. As Lieutenant Commander Willink began to implement his vision of how each platoon would conduct their operations, he realized there was a decision to make. He called in the platoons for a briefing.

He explained that he wanted to send a platoon over to the eastern side of Ramadi and that doing so would give TU Bruiser the ability to maneuver swiftly anywhere within the city for any direct-action operations. The eastern base, however, known as Camp Corrigedor, was dilapidated and run down. The building they would be staying in had dirt floors, a tin roof, and was in terrible condition.

Willink left the decision up to the men and walked out of the room. One by one, Michael, along with every single Delta Platoon member, stood up, walked over to the whiteboard on the wall, and wrote his name on it. They were a single, cohesive war-fighting unit and volunteered to go as such. The previous months of training and living together bonded them like brothers.

THIRTEEN

Camp Corregidor, Ar Ramadi, Iraq, 2006

The army captain sat peacefully in silence in one of the only places set apart from the chaos and violence that was now Ramadi, Iraq. He was a little old for the rank of captain, but that was not uncommon for a person with his specific duties within the military. He had spent years in formation and training, and was now here in the thick of the Battle of Ramadi. The quiet was broken by a firm knock at the door. The man arose from his seat and moved to answer it. He opened the door to find a tall, brown-eyed, dark-haired young man patiently waiting. "Are you a Catholic priest?"

"I am," replied Father Halladay.

"Nice to meet you. I am a Catholic and my name is Michael Monsoor. I'd like to go to confession."

Father Halladay grabbed his stole and motioned Michael to follow him.

Father Paul Halladay was forty years old at the time of his deployment to Ramadi and was an army chaplain in the 1st Battalion, 506th Infantry Regiment, 101st Airborne Division (1st of the 506th). His main mission was to assist the soldiers of Camp Corregidor to worship according to their own religion and preference but was ordained a Catholic priest and was happy to oblige Michael's request for confession.

They sat down in the makeshift chapel. Michael had just arrived in Ramadi, and Father Halladay understood well the situation the men were facing on a daily basis. He thought it showed significant religious formation and conviction for Michael to seek him out after only recently arriving in Ramadi.

When Father Halladay arrived on Camp Corregidor just a few months prior in November 2005, the building he was working in had been an agricultural school building. The room now being used as the chapel was previously a classroom with a tin roof. Because of the frequency that the building was hit with indirect fire, they needed to reenforce the ceiling and walls with sandbags inside and out. Father Halladay had inherited the room from a Protestant chaplain and found the holy tabernacle, which Catholic priests use to hold the true body and blood of Christ, on the floor in the corner. There was a SpongeBob SquarePants sheet hanging on one of the walls, and the room had little seating available for Mass. He knew he must get right to work.

He enlisted some talented Seabees, the tradesmen of the US Navy. These are the men and women that, when needed, will go into harm's way to build, wire, plumb, frame, and maintain the structures and equipment used by other service members and, if the situation dictates, all while wearing body armor and carrying a rifle. Their contributions to the success of military operations cannot be overstated. In the end they provided the chapel with around a dozen pews so people would have a place to sit, as well as reenforced the pillars that held up the ceiling so it would not cave in the next time an enemy mortar fell too close for comfort.

Father Halladay found other talent to help as well. One of the soldiers, Manny, had been a comic book artist and was commissioned to draw the Stations of the Cross on the walls of the chapel. He didn't disappoint; he drew each of the fourteen stations in charcoal throughout the entire room. Father Halladay set up a red sanctuary lamp, signifying the presence of Christ when lit, that he had received from the Knights of Columbus order back home. He placed the tabernacle on a stand alongside a chalice to hold the wine. He pulled down the SpongeBob SquarePants sheet and replaced it with green drapes he found while going through boxes in one of the rooms. They were not perfect but not too tattered or ripped to be used for the chapel walls. Finally, and most importantly, he consecrated the bread into Christ's body for any soul who may need it in this grave and unforgiving war.

Because of the warfighters' operating tempo, they were in and out of camp a lot. Father Halladay held daily Mass and encouraged anyone to come if they hadn't been able to make it in a while. If they couldn't make it to Sunday Mass, he told them any day would work. Michael came to Mass whenever he could, and Father Halladay was always checking in on Michael when he ran into him. He knew the intensity of the SEALs' schedule, and he wanted Michael to know he was there any time he needed anything, but most importantly, any time he needed the sacraments of confession and the Eucharist.

Each warfighter dealt with the reality of war and their role in it differently. What these service members were tasked with day in and day out was a reality that most human beings will never face much less ever volunteer to face. One of those warfighters, R.R., has this to say on the matter:

"The vast majority of people do not understand the mindset of those who say they desire to go to war. Those who express that desire do not actually know themselves if they do until they are there. Of those, even fewer have a desire to ever return. War is not some glorious thing that creates heroes and legends. It is a grotesque example of what human beings will do to each other in the absence of civility. Overwhelmingly, those who willingly return desire not war itself but to recompense and punish, to seek justice with the end goal of peace. The prize is not glory or recognition; it is the satisfaction in bringing punishment to the bad, recompense to the victim, and justice to all. However great and noble that sounds in words, it is terrible and often costly in action. It means that some good men will step out of civilized society intending to go into harm's way, to commit acts of violence on behalf of those who will not, in efforts to accomplish what is good and just. The consequence of these noble actions is death for many of those involved. The outcome of the endeavor is tragic and sad, often society is shielded from the gore in exchange for the glory, but just as sleep is the brother of death, glory is the brother of gore. The virtuous who really understand this will never glorify the exploits of war, will never seek to gain from their part in it, will never desire war for the sake of war, but will instead put themselves in the path of the unjust using violence and death to preserve the lives of the innocent and the civil societies from which they come. It is likely that the general population will never understand the minority who have this mindset. Many say they want justice for all yet never stop to contemplate what that actually means.

"As George Orwell pointed out, people sleep peacefully in their beds at night only because rough men stand ready to do violence on their behalf."[1]

FOURTEEN

"Gabriel, this is your grandmother," Michael said as he imitated a squeaky, elderly woman's voice to his roommate and good friend, Gabe Lynch, via satellite phone. Gabe laughed on the other end realizing it was Michael up to his usual antics.

"How is it going, bro? Are you guys crushing it out there right now?" Gabe asked, still home in the States, his team being next to head out on deployment.

"A little," Michael responded ambiguously. Michael was not one to ever speak highly of himself and always preferred to leave more unsaid than said, but just as he was about to change the subject, his teammate Tommy D. piped in over his shoulder.

"Gabe! He saved K.'s life. It was crazy!"

Gabe smiled to himself; he was not surprised. Michael was never the one to cower when it was time to step up. He loved hearing their stories as he knew Ramadi was crawling with terrorist insurgents and was proud to know his friends were holding it down.

It was early May and the guys had been at Camp Corregidor for just over a month. Sweat poured down Michael's face, and he could still hear the HMMWVs in the distance. K. was now out of immediate danger, but Michael and his fire team were not and continued to move from cover to cover while returning fire. The IA (Iraqi Army) partners had also joined the fight, and with definite overwhelming force, the SEALs and IA bounded safely out of the firefight.

Michael's fire team returned to base to debrief and begin the after action report (AAR). It was there that the rest of Delta Platoon found out about Michael's immediate and fearless action to protect K. Michael had said nothing, but it was clear how angry he was that K. had been shot. For K., it was a flight back to the States for surgery and rehab. Yet, all the while, he intended to heal up and get back into the fight alongside his brothers. He kept saying he'd see them shortly. The guys knew better. Unfortunately, with an injury like his, K. would not be able to return. It was weird to send a teammate home, especially so soon. The perception of "It happens to other units but not us" was shattered. They were in the middle of intense firefights on almost a daily basis, and this was the first injury. The operating tempo they were facing required hyperfocus, and the guys, completely undeterred, stepped up and went to work.

"We asked a lot of our guys, especially with the number of missions we were conducting while facing extreme heat, dehydration, and exhaustion. It didn't faze them; they all stepped up and performed," Mike Sarraille, Michael's assistant officer in charge, said.

Mike and his teammates were beginning to find their rhythm together. Delta Platoon had been broken up into two squads, with their OIC (officer in charge), Seth Stone, leading one squad and Mike Sarraille leading the other squad, which Michael was in. There were army and marine units also stationed in Ramadi that the SEALs were providing assistance to, one of the large army battalions being the 1st of the 506th. This unit was descended from the "Band of Brothers" unit from World War II. The battalion was huge and led by Lieutenant Colonel Ron Clark. His men were professional, talented, and worked incredibly well with the SEALs.

Michael's troop commander, Lieutenant Commander Jocko Willink, had instructed his men to use the army's uniform: a tricolor gray digital pattern called the Army Combat Uniform, or ACU. It was very different from the tricolor desert Naval Special Warfare Uniform. The men wore it with little complaint and even shaved their heads to match their army brethren. This not only increased the cohesion of the two units but also had a very practical purpose. By blending in with the army unit, the SEALs did not stand out as special forces. The enemy had begun to target soldiers that looked or dressed differently than the average GI. By this point in the war, the SEAL teams and other special forces groups were beginning to become a real problem for the insurgency due not only to the men associated with these teams but also because they had a huge amount of backside support personnel. This support took intelligence specialists and combat enablers that would find and fix a target location so the special operators could finish it. It was a three-step process (Find, Fix, Finish) that involves finding the enemy, getting a fix on their physical location, and then sending a special operations unit to finish the target by capturing or killing the enemy there.

The order of battle for the SEALs would largely consist of word coming from the army forty-eight hours ahead of time informing them on what area of Ramadi they would be patrolling. The SEALs would then plan and provide sniper overwatch during the army patrol.

By this point, the two units worked well together, and the men of Delta had settled in and were acclimated to life on Camp Corregidor. They had accomplished a lot in only one month. When Michael and the guys of Delta first arrived and saw the unfinished and dilapidated camp along with the bombed-out building they had all volunteered to live in, they knew they needed to get right to work. The platoon brought in shipments of plywood and two-by-fours along with all the hardware and tools they would need to build up and fortify their new home. The floors were still dirt and in a couple of months would turn to mud with the fall rain. The tin roof would be noisy and provided little protection, and the walls were shaky at best. Even after making those repairs, it would only keep the building from falling down with the next mortar attack, much less house an operational platoon of SEALs. The men had quite a bit of work ahead of them to make it a safe and fortified living space.

Even amid their overloaded operating schedule, the men of Delta Platoon gathered the supplies to build a home away from home of the tattered building where they would be spending the deployment. They nicknamed it "Full Metal Jacket" due to its similarity to the bombed-out buildings of Hue city in the movie of the same name.

A plywood floor was laid, and the walls were reinforced with sandbags. Foam was then sprayed between the inner and outer layers for insulation. They framed and built out rooms for each man and installed a small A/C unit to help cool the air but mostly to keep the air moving. In certain parts of the building, the men needed to watch their step in order to avoid exposed rebar. The heat was miserable in May, reaching upwards of 115 degrees, and fixing up and finishing "Full Metal Jacket" was a welcome reprieve. The men of Delta Platoon had made this once barely standing building a home away from home: by normal standards nothing to write home about but nonetheless a haven in the midst of chaos and heat.

"We were living in war poverty, but we had each other, and we loved every minute of it," remembers Mike Sarraille.

As the men continued to work on their rooms, a loud voice yelled into the building: "We've got an op; get it on!"

FIFTEEN

Michael grabbed his Mk 48 and headed swiftly to the ready room. There he met up with the rest of his platoon. Mike reached into his cubby and grabbed his armor, helmet, and radio. As he pulled his armor over his head, he thought about what he needed to load up into his backpack for the mission. They would be assisting the Iraqi Army scouts and US Army Gunfighter Company in a daytime patrol through the southern Ramadi Malaab district. The SEALs would provide flank security for both elements during the foot patrol.

It was midmorning and the temperature was already intensely hot. Michael knew he would need to have extra water, but he also knew he'd need additional ammo besides what he already carried in his AW ammo pouches.

He had to decide what he needed more; he chose the ammo. One bottle of water would have to suffice.

After loading up his backpack, he reached into his cubby and grabbed his gun belt that held his 9-millimeter Sig Saur pistol and Velcroed it around his waist. He then secured two drop leg holster straps around his thigh and checked his touch points, a practice many warfighters do to ensure their equipment is in the exact position that they expect it to be without having to think twice about it. He looked into his cubby one last time to make sure he had everything he needed.

Before he left the ready room, he grabbed his fire team leader and asked him to do a quick gear check. "I've got my helmet, NODS, armor, radio, gun, ammo, water."

"Yep, good to go. Let's roll," responded Chief Fortin.

Mike and the platoon headed out to the vehicles where they would circle up and do comms checks. Each man keyed up his push-to-talk and checked in with the lead communicator. Once every man was good, they loaded the trucks and rolled out.

Fifteen minutes later, they arrived at the area of operation.

The tac-lead's voice broke over the radio: "Fives and twenty-fives, guys."

The turret gunner scanned the immediate area around their vehicles out to twenty-five yards to ensure there were no IED's or other hazardous objects in the vicinity. All of the vehicles checked in; the area was clear.

"Dismount, dismount, dismount," instructed a voice over the radio.

Mike strapped on his helmet and got out of the vehicle. He did a quick scan of the buildings surrounding them and moved to his position in the patrol. The combined team began to mobilize and move through the street. They continued through multiple sectors of the Malaab district unopposed, heading west.

Bababba . . . bababba . . . bababba . . . The deafening noise of machine gun fire suddenly erupted from an enemy insurgent position to the right.

Michael dropped into his field of fire and, identifying the enemy position, immediately sent back a long burst with his Mk 48.

"Contact right," multiple SEALs yelled as they sent round after round toward the enemy.

Mike sprinted to the closest position of cover, which was a courtyard wall of a nearby house, and picked up the fire. The other SEALs and Iraqi Army scouts moved into the courtyard and began to return fire as well. "Changing!" yelled Michael as he stripped out an empty ammo box and loaded a full one. Just as he closed the feed tray cover, five enemy fighters moved to flank Michael and his team. "They are flanking to the west!" Mike yelled as he fired at the maneuvering insurgents. He caught them halfway through their movement and had them pinned behind a small vehicle.

"Hold them there, Mike!" J. P. yelled.

Mike could overhear the Marine Air Naval Gunfire Liaison Company (ANGLICO) guys on the radio setting up for a strike on the enemy fighters he had pinned down.

"This will be a type two control . . . 1-3 N/A, line four 1,6,0, feet . . . five enemy fighters behind a white sedan . . . 5,0,0 meters north of the stadium . . . enemy marked by red smoke . . . friendlies 3,2,0 meters east no mark . . . egress to the overhead . . . make your attack heading 0,1,0 +/- ten, request 1 x GBU-38 and 20 millimeter. Approved for immediate push, say when in."

"Copy all, contact red smoke and white sedan, tally target. Dash two will be in first with guns, dash one will follow with 1 x GBU," replied the pilot.

Mike listened as the controller finished. He knew he would need to keep the enemy pinned until the F/A-18s could drop.

"CAS in at +30," called out the controller letting the guys know that the jets were thirty seconds out from dropping.

For Michael, this seemed like an eternity. He had the best vantage point to keep the enemy where they were as the other SEALs and scouts were still engaging the original enemy position. He conserved his ammo knowing a reload may give the insurgents just enough time to maneuver away from their current position, which could cause the close air support (CAS) strike to have to abort and start over. He continued to send five- to eight-round bursts into the vehicle.

Babababababa . . . babababababababa!

He was not going to let a single one of them continue to flank their position. Michael had only a couple of bursts left before he would have to reload when he heard one of the ANGLICO marines yell, "Guns! Guns! Guns!"

Michael sent a long burst into the car, then immediately following heard the unmistakable sound of the F/A-18's 20-millimeter Gatling gun. *Brrrrrrr . . . Brrrrrrr!* The dirt and asphalt exploded around the vehicle as the rounds impacted the area. Mike stripped his empty box and reloaded.

"One away, ten seconds to impact," called out the controller.

The dust was heavy, but Michael could still see enough to know that none of the five enemy soldiers had left the position. Suddenly, a flash, then the car ripped apart and disappeared in a cloud of black and gray smoke.

"Good hits, stand by for BDA [Battle Damage Assessment]," stated the controller over the radio. The dust cleared. Where the sedan used to be was a crater with indistinguishable metal debris and other material scattered in the area. Michael could make out three of the five enemy soldiers, now lying in peculiar positions near the blast site.

"Good hits 5 x EKIA!" Michael heard the controller say. The original enemy position went quiet immediately after the strike. The SEALs, marines, and scouts maneuvered to assess and secure the building. The scouts entered and cleared it only to find that the enemy had left the area.

"All right, guys, there is nothing here. Let's Charlie, Mike [CM: continue mission]," said Chief Fortin, and the SEALs and scouts moved to reestablish their security position for the main element.

SIXTEEN

Michael climbed up the hand-built wooden ladder steps to his bunk and moved his extra pillows aside to get into his bed. He was exhausted and ready for a few hours of sleep. He stretched his sore muscles and began to doze off. The long hours, patrols, and heavy equipment were beginning to wear on his body.

He had a sign on his room door that said, "Mikey's Palace." His room was the center of activity on many nights. The guys loved coming by because he always had an unending stash of food: stuffed olives, jerky, and ramen noodles. He hung up bright tapestries from his brother back home and was usually awake odd hours of the evening. Not tonight, though; tonight he was spent. He had only a few hours before he needed to prep for their next operation.

The annoying buzz of Mike's alarm clock pulled him out of what seemed like a great dream, but he couldn't quite remember. Mike hopped out of bed, grabbed his gun, and headed for the ready room.

Looking up at the brightest star he could find, Michael adjusted his night vision. As always, the night sky looked unreal through his "NODS" (night vision optics device). There were so many more stars visible than the naked eye could see. As the rest of the guys dismounted the truck, Michael moved off to one side of the road careful to step over and around the trash and debris in the area. His eighteen-man patrol was tasked as a bounding overwatch for an Iraqi Army clearance in the Malaab district of Ramadi.

It was just after midnight, but it was not quiet or still. Distant gun shots and strings of automatic weapon fire could be heard across the city. Mike scanned the rooftops and second stories of the buildings across from him, his Mk 48 resting against his armor plate. It would take less than a second for Michael to raise it and fire in the event that they were contacted from the surrounding buildings.

The men continued on for around a mile without incident and reached their final overwatch position, where they would stay until extract.

As they approached the multistory house, the Iraqi scouts entered first to clear and gain control of the occupants. As the scouts marshaled and secured the family inside, the SEALs entered and conducted a final clearance.

"Target secure," Mike Sarraille whispered over the radio.

Michael and his fire team went to the rooftop to set up their security positions. He prepped his individual position and laid out his extra ammo in the event he needed quick access to the extra boxes. Michael found some cardboard on the roof and set it up as a shade to cover him from the penetrating sun that would soon be rising. The hours passed as the Iraqi Army continued their clearance below.

The sky began to lighten as the sun approached the horizon.

"I've got movement in the alleyway," whispered J. P.

Michael scanned his field of fire. "Nothing here," he replied. Just as Michael finished the last syllable, another team member fired.

"Contact to the east one block away. Five MAMs [military age males] maneuvering to the north. I just lost them behind the houses," the team member yelled.

Immediately, enemy fire began to hit the wall around the rooftop. Michael repositioned toward the contact and fired. The enemy were using the cover of the surrounding houses effectively and continued to harass the security position. It was clear this was not like other attacks. It was well coordinated. The enemy was careful not to engage from the same spot for too long and continued to maneuver and flank. The rounds from Mike's 48 began to eat chunks out of the corners and ledges that the enemy were using as cover. The short rooftop wall was beginning to degrade as well, however, and bullets were penetrating the plaster in some areas. The men stayed low and continued to engage. Michael was glad he had prepped his extra ammo ahead of time. It looked as though he would be needing it soon.

Michael and the other SEALs on the rooftop were not the only ones taking fire. The IA scouts were trying to exit the house to maneuver on the insurgents but were pinned inside. Every time one of the scouts tried to exit the house, a hail of bullets hit the area around the exit. On the rooftop the situation was not improving, and it looked like ammunition might soon become a problem. Not for Michael—he continued to engage multiple enemy positions stopping only to reload and reposition.

"Mikey! How's your ammo?" yelled J. P.

"I'm good to go!"

"Damn, bro, carrying all that extra weight might save all our lives!" J. P. smiled but was really dead serious. Michael's 48 continued to eat away at the enemy positions. An indistinct yell came from the right. Michael turned to see one of the enemy insurgents try to cross the street toward the SEALs' position. He sent a burst, and the enemy fighter fell against the hot pavement, motionless.

With this, the momentum changed, and Michael moved from position to position engaging the enemy on three sides. He was the only AW (automatic weapon gunner) on the roof, and although the other SEALs were holding their own well, a 5.56-millimeter M4 doesn't have quite the same effect as a 7.62-millimeter belt-fed machine gun.

The enemy was losing and it began to show. The volume of incoming fire had drastically decreased and was much more sporadic until only one enemy position was still active. The SEALs and scouts concentrated fire on the spot. The area went quiet, and the men waited for another attack. But it never came. In all, Michael had fired more than six hundred rounds of ammunition and was likely the reason that the security position was not overrun. Seven enemy lay dead without one SEAL or scout injured.

"Hey, Dad, it's Mike." Michael spoke happily into the satellite phone. He had just returned from an op and after showering and changing out of his gear, he dialed home to check in.

"Mikeys, how are you doing?"

"I'm good, Dad, we are still training Iraqi forces. I'm pretty bored here. What's new at home?" Michael was careful to not go into any detail about the true nature of work they were conducting on a daily basis. He didn't want his parents to worry. He preferred to keep the amount of danger they faced to himself.

As George and Michael discussed his gear and weapons, Sally walked over to George. She was eager to hear

Michael's voice. She had barely spoken to him since he left because every time he called, she made sure her children and husband had ample time with Michael on the phone first. She was also busy finishing up a master's degree in counseling, marriage, and family therapy, so any amount of time she had to speak with Michael, she treasured. Michael never discussed any of his combat operations with her; she knew he wanted to protect her from worrying. But she also knew better. She had walked past the hallway when her sons were on their computer looking at photos of Michael patrolling through the streets, and she instantly knew: he was facing a grave enemy day in and day out. She couldn't be there, but she could pray, and that she did. She prayed the rosary, a collection of prayers based upon the life of Christ and honoring His Blessed Mother, whom warfighters have credited assisting them in epic battles throughout history, such as the Battle of Lepanto as well as the Battle of New Orleans and countless others. Sally wasn't seeking anything grand with her prayers. She simply requested protection for her son as she prayed it every single day.

It was now Sally's turn to speak to Michael, and she held the phone tightly to her ear so she could hear her son clearly. "How are you, Mike? I miss you! Did you receive the care packages we sent to you? We really enjoyed making them for you and your teammates!"

"They were great, Mom, thank you. Even the package full of female toiletries you and your friends threw in there." Mike chuckled. "Not sure who will use that one, but we got a kick out of it. I appreciate you and everyone taking the time to think of us. The packages will definitely go to good use, Mom."

"I'm so glad, honey," Sally responded with a big grin on her face.

"I'm gonna head to bed now, but I wanted to say hello to you guys." Mike's voice began to drift off. The day's operation had begun to hit him like a wall, and his body was just now registering the need for sleep.

"Of course, take care of yourself. We are all okay here, Michael. Stay focused so you can come home safe," Sally said. Those words became her parting words every time she spoke to him: "Stay focused so you can come home safe."

SEVENTEEN

Malaab District, Ar Ramadi, Iraq,
July 22, 2006

The cool water felt nice going down Michael's throat. The moon dust that covered so much of Iraq was an irritant to say the least; the fine dust floated through the air and permeated almost everything. He gargled and spit in the corner of the rooftop. He and his team had just taken the target house that they would be temporarily using for overwatch for the Iraqi battalion's disruption operation.

Michael wiped the sweat off of his face and removed his backpack. Just as he began to unzip the main compartment to start prepping his extra ammo, he looked at the black splotches where big block letters used to spell out *Monsoor.* The only distinguishable character was the hastily covered letter *M*, but just to the left was something else, something faded but unmistakable for those of the same profession. Michael reached into his pocket and withdrew a black Sharpie. He traced over the faded image. First, the circle, then the dashes perpendicular to the circumference at twelve, three, six, and nine o'clock. Finally, a single central dot finished the image. Michael used this in place of his name. In the event the enemy was ever able to get hold of his belongings, they would not have the name of the owner. It was a reticle, specific to the gunsight often used by special operators during that time and now widely used throughout the firearms industry. Really, for Mike, it was not just an identifier for his gear; it was also a reminder to stay focused and sharp. In addition, Michael wanted to attend the prestigious NSW Sniper Course after the deployment. Michael replaced the cap back onto his Sharpie, put it back in his pocket, and finished unzipping his bag.

"Mikey, pack up, we are moving," called his team leader from across the roof.

Michael zipped up his bag, pulled it over his shoulders, and grabbed his gun.

Michael broke the corner and held long down the street. Another SEAL stepped close and gently bumped him, letting Michael know that he was good to move across. Michael quickly moved to the next position, a courtyard wall with a large hole blown out of the corner that would allow him to stay in cover while also providing security down the street he had just crossed, facilitating the rest of the squad to move across themselves. The new target house was slightly down the road to

Michael's left. The recce (reconnaissance) team had already set up to contain the house, and the rest of the guys who made up the main assault force were moving into position to make entry.

Being an AW, Mike was not normally part of the main entry. This time was no different, and he held a security position back in the direction they had just come from. The recce team had climbed an adjacent house and was covering the rooftop of the target house along with the road opposite of Michael. Behind him, the others moved into place. When security was set on the windows and back side, the breach team began moving to the door. Breachers are team members that gain entry into the target for the main entry team and have extra training in using tools and techniques from lockpicks to explosives to perform the task. In this case, the breacher was accompanied by another SEAL for security in case someone inside opened the door while the breacher was working. For these disruption operations, the team along with the IA were going to clear through areas known for enemy activity. Ramadi, however, was a large city, and it was difficult as the enemy had a myriad of means to find out what was happening and move before the clearance took place.

The radio crackled. "Turning steel!" the breacher yelled. A moment later there was a loud blast. "Open, open, open!" was the next thing he yelled, indicating that the door was open and the entry team could take the first room.

The one man entered, checked his corner, and scanned the room. He was followed by the two, three, and four man, each clearing his sector of the room. It looked to be the living room.

"Clear . . . All clear," the men called to each other.

The rest of the assault force flowed into the first room and began stacking on the other doors and entries that led into the rest of the house. Michael was the last off the street other than the recce team that would stay in place until the target was fully cleared and secure.

The SEALs moved from room to room. Michael found the stairwell that led to the second story and held up there while the others continued clearing rooms on the first floor. Michael felt a hand grab the back of his armor and give a gentle tug. "Back up just a few steps, Mikey," another SEAL whispered. The guys were about to make entry into a room just across from where Michael was standing and didn't want to open the door with him standing in front of it.

Michael stepped back and against the adjacent wall. This put him in a position out of the way but still with a clear view up the stairs. The men opened the door and entered. Michael gave it a few seconds just in case any shooting started and moved back to his original position. Within seconds, he felt a hand squeeze his inner thigh. This was a nonverbal signal for him to start moving up the stairs and that there were enough guys behind him to take the second floor.

Michael ascended the stairs, but he did not stop at the second floor. There was one more flight leading up to a cupola that exited onto the roof. Michael moved into the stairwell and let the rest of the team swiftly flow behind him into a short hallway that led to the remaining rooms on the second floor. Michael felt a squeeze and he began to move. He could see the door that led to the roof, and although the snipers in the recce element had cleared the rooftop, it was not uncommon to have people in that small area of the cupola. Michael scanned the edge of the landing looking for any movement. As he ascended, it became apparent that the area was clear. The SEALs prepared to exit onto the roof.

"Frogmen going external, rooftop, target building," one of the men called over the radio. They paused to ensure the sniper element received the call, then opened the door and made entry onto the rooftop. As expected, the rooftop was clear and a radio call was made that the target was clear and the men could move to security positions.

"Target secure. All right, guys, let's get to work," Chief Fortin called over the radio.

The snipers began getting their firing positions set up. Because of the extreme heat, guys would bring or find material to set up for shade. When the work was complete, the squad settled into their positions to cover the Iraqi Army clearance.

Michael looked around at all of the debris, rocks, and crumbled buildings. The enemy could be hiding anywhere in the chaos. He leaned against the dusty rooftop wall that stood a short three feet in height. As he pulled his extra ammo from his bag, he reached in for one other item he had brought. When they had begun the deployment a few months prior, it quickly became apparent how dangerous it was to hold security while looking over a wall. Michael had a solution to this problem. He emailed his sister, Sara, a few weeks prior letting her know to expect a care package and asked if she would ship it to him as soon as she received it.[1] Michael pulled a cylinder from his bag.

"Hey, Mikey, what is that?" asked one of the guys.

Michael held it up proudly. "It's a periscope." The men laughed as Michael extended it and looked over the wall. There was a warm breeze that kicked up the dust. In addition, it brought with it the distinct smell of burning trash and smoke from the burn pits, a practice that was common due to the lack of sanitation infrastructure and landfills. The day was still clear enough to see into the distance, but the dust and smoke gave the air and sky an orange hue.

The Iraqi Army clearance continued as the SEALs looked for enemy movement.

Snap, snap . . . snap, snap, snap! The men stayed low and shifted from behind the loopholes as the incoming fire hit the building and snapped overhead.

"Where are they at!?" one of the men yelled.

Michael peered through his periscope. The guys weren't laughing now. As he scanned, he could see dust kick up from multiple positions. The gunfire picked up; the men could hear it hitting the side of the building. Rounds were coming through the windows and even the small loopholes on the rooftop wall. The guys waited for a lull, then fired back into the enemy positions, but the enemy were dug in well. Michael sent burst after burst, and every time, the firing stopped just long enough for the SEALs to reposition and engage.

"We are breaking contact and moving to extract!" came the team leader's voice over the radio.

Michael knew that there would be no way for them to safely move off of the roof and out of the house without him laying down suppressive covering fire into the enemy positions.

"Let's move, guys!" one of the SEALs on the rooftop yelled.

Without a thought, Michael grabbed his bag full of ammo and ran to the side of the house taking the most effective fire. He crouched as he propped his Mk 48 on the top of the roof wall and began to fire. His long bursts peppered the enemy position as the other SEALs moved to the cupola and down to the first floor.

"Mikey, let's go, bro!" his teammate yelled.

"If I stop, the guys will have no covering fire for their movement!"

"Got you, bro! I'll let the others know that we will move to them!" his teammate yelled from the cupola stairs. Michael's gun went dry. He grabbed another box and began to load. The enemy fire picked up again.

Michael stood up and moved to another position on the rooftop as he finished loading. The enemy redirected their fire away from the maneuvering SEALs and back onto Michael's position on the rooftop.

"Mikey, be careful. You're pretty exposed up there, man!" the other SEAL yelled.

Michael knew it was a risk staying on the roof, but it was by far the best position to cover his teammates as they moved. Having a fresh box in his gun, Michael sent a liberal burst in answer to the incoming enemy fire. Enemy rounds continued to hit the rooftop wall. Small pieces of plaster and concrete exploded off the wall with every round. It seemed like every enemy position was shooting at him, but he was not going to leave until he knew the other guys had made it to the safety of cover.

The radio crackled: "Mikey, get your ass off that rooftop; we will cover your movement to us!" came Chief Fortin's voice over comms.

Michael sent one more long burst, dropped low, and moved into the house. He met Rey who was holding rear security, and they moved together to the door. The men looked at each other. "You ready?" Michael asked his friend.

"Yah, bro, let's move." He keyed up his radio and called to the rest of the waiting guys. "Moving to you, exiting the target now."

The pair bounded from cover to cover until they finally reached the other waiting SEALs. The group moved anther two blocks away without incident to the waiting extract vehicles and returned to camp. It was not apparent what Michael had done until the adrenaline rush subsided. It was then that the guys realized Michael had selflessly risked his own safety in order to cover their movement off the roof and out of the enemy field of fire—a feat that may not have ended well without Michael staying on the rooftop.

EIGHTEEN

creech . . . screeeech . . . raaaaaargh.

Chris Kimbrell jerked his head toward his door and thought, "What the heck is that?"

The door creaked as it slowly opened. Chris stared intently as it moved. The glow from the movie he was watching was not bright enough to see clearly and, if anything, made the situation even more creepy. He could see a dark object moving across the threshold near the bottom of the door. His eyes finally began to adjust to the darkness.

Mike was down on one knee with his head cocked and slowly peeked farther into the room. Chris squinted and could just make out Mike's sly half smile.

"What are you doing, you turd," Chris said as Mike's face broke into a full-sized grin. Mike stood up and stepped into the room. He was still wearing his full kit, armor, h-gear, and ammo; he had come right to Chris's room from the previous op. He gave Chris a big hug, which actually hurt a bit because of all the edges of Mike's equipment.

"What's up, bro?"

"How was the op?" Chris asked.

"It went well enough. The fighting is getting heavy, but my AW is humming. Hey, I know you're all into your movie, but do you want to go get a workout in?"

"Ahh yah, bro, I'm down."

"Okay, I'll meet you over there. I'm going to stop by medical; my ear is killing me."

"Sounds good."

———

The barbell clanged as Michael finished his set and placed it back on the rack.

"What's up with your ear, dude?" Chris asked.

"A rough ear infection. They are sending me to TQ to get some treatment."

Chris was over in Ramadi with Team 8 who were conducting operations of their own. In his and Mike's downtime, the BUD/S classmates and friends were able to catch up and hang out.

"How's everything on your side?" asked Michael.

"Ops are good, been going back and forth with family at home though. They don't get it."

"Yeah, I know. I have friends from home asking me to bring them back souvenirs, and my brother is not happy with me for one reason or another. I'm running through the fucking streets getting shot at and all I can think of is, 'I need to call my brother and make up with my family.'"

"I hear you. It is hard to explain to people back home what is really going on here."

The friends continued to talk of family and home along with the recent firefight that claimed the life of Marc Lee and left Ryan Job permanently blinded. As they finished up the last few sets, they agreed it was best if they called home to ensure there was nothing left unsaid. Michael thanked Chris for being up for the workout and talk, and the men left each other to make their calls.

Losing Marc had a profound effect on the guys. Until then, no SEAL had been killed during the fighting in Iraq. Every day in Iraq there were soldiers and marines coming in maimed or killed, but not the Team Guys. Sure, there had been injuries, but nothing like Marc Lee or Ryan Job. The idea of "It happens to other units, not us," faded into "That could have been me."

"Not many people talk about what happens after a teammate is killed, at least not in a public setting. There is disbelief, anger, a sense of vulnerability, sadness. These are expected or can at least be surmised by even those who have never had the experience," a SEAL somberly described. "But what is largely unknown is the physical work done by those warfighters left after their fallen have been taken home. The cleaning of the gear and equipment so that the service member's loved ones are not subject to the gore of what a battlefield death so often looks like. The meticulous inventorying and packing of their teammate's personal belongings. It physically hurts to walk into a friend's room to close the book they had left open just a few hours before, to remove his bedding and pillow, to pack his shoes and clothes, to only now notice all of the things that were unique to this particular person and that describe without words who they were. This is almost always done by those who lived and fought next to him and often leaves these warfighters with an impression that they will carry for the rest of their lives."

———

Rey pointed a small video camera around the rooftop. The sun had just begun to brighten the sky enough for the camera to pick up a decent image. Rey stopped at Mike as he prepped his cardboard box that would be his structure protecting him from the searing Levant sun.

"There's Mike. What's up, Mike?"

"What's up, ese?" Mike responded with a laugh.

They were well into another overwatch and the army would be arriving at the area soon to begin the clearance. Any minute, Adhan would begin, the Salat al-fajr. This is the first of five daily prayer times practiced in

Islam. The minaret loudspeakers crackled and seconds later the call to prayer began. "Allahu Akbar! Allahu Akbar! Allahu Akbar! Allahu Akbar! Ashhadu alla ilaha illallah . . ."

Michael gave his best attempt to follow along. "Alll—ahalaahahalbabab."

It was the fifteenth of August. The IA along with the US Army would be conducting clearance of another portion of the Malaab district. The houses were tightly packed and clearance would likely be slow. The SEALs came prepared and were all set with cardboard shade, water, and a ton of extra ammunition. The men didn't know it, but soon they would have no need for the shade.

As the call to prayer ended, Michael scanned the surrounding area with his periscope. He glanced over to see his teammates to the right, each with their own as well. He smiled and continued to scan. It had worked out so well for Michael that a bunch of the guys had them sent out.

"Nothing to see over here, guys. Just the IA and army dudes getting unloaded," Michael called.

Then the loudspeakers crackled on. "That's weird," thought Michael. It seemed as though the prayers were going to start again. A voice came over the loudspeakers, but it sounded different this time. It was not the usual singing; it was speaking and the words were different.

"What is that? Are they praying again? That doesn't sound like daily prayer," Chief Fortin said.

"I know. It's not the same," Michael responded.

The interpreter burst through the cupola door and onto the roof.

"It's directions. They are being directed!" he blurted out.

"What? Who?" asked Chief Fortin.

"The speakers; the enemy fighters are being directed on where to go," the interpreter replied.

"Oh, well, shit. J. P., Doug, Mike, do any of you have a shot to take out those speakers?" called Chief Fortin. But the snipers had already been trying to work a solution.

"No joy, Chief," was the response.

"Mikey, I hope you brought a lot of ammo. Shit's probably going to get real stupid, real quick," said Chief Fortin.

"Always."

"They are directing them to our position," called the interpreter. He had stayed on the roof to give the guys any updates.

Mike Sarraille keyed up his radio and called to the lead communicator. "Get on the horn with the army and ensure they are tracking what's going on. We have enemy inbound to our position."

"The army is tracking. They have already been engaged," the communicator called back.

Rey began to fire. "I've got enemy maneuvering to the west," Rey said.

The snipers were seeing movement as well, and Michael shifted his position to look toward the west. The enemy had not started to fire back yet and were using the rubble and blown-out buildings for cover as they moved closer to the overwatch position. The guys were having a hard time getting a good shot, and with the guidance from the speakers, the enemy were moving in a much more organized pattern. It was apparent that they knew exactly where the SEALs were.

Pop, pop, pop! Pieces of the side of the house burst off in different directions. The insurgents began the assault from the south and, immediately after, a PK machine gun lit up from the west. Michael fired back to the west as the others engaged to the south. The speaker was still blaring, and from the distant gunfire, it sounded as if the other units were still in the fight as well.

Comms chattered, but most of it was not pertinent to Michael. It was mostly information flow from the different units' leaders to each other and back to the Joint Operations Center where the operation was being monitored. Michael's concern was keeping the enemy pinned and if one of them was brave enough to try to move into the open, dropping him in his tracks.

The clearance was ongoing, but the insurgents currently attacking the SEAL position were relentless and not providing any of the men a clear shot. This was not ideal, but it also meant that they were not trying to advance toward the overwatch position. It had been hours and neither side could get the upper hand. The JTAC continued to help the supporting aircraft try to get a solution, but due to the proximity to friendlies and the civilian population, he could not allow the aircraft to drop ordnance.

Michael moved from position to position, firing at multiple enemy locations. It looked as though this fight was not going to be over any time soon, and he wasn't wrong. Although the guys were able to get a clear shot here and there, the enemy positions were well protected. When the battle finally ended and the post-engagement BDA (Battle Damage Assessment) was complete, the men found seven enemy fighters KIA (killed in action). The actual number was likely double as many of the locals would drag their dead away. This was because cultural norms required burial of the dead before sundown. The entire engagement had lasted twelve hours.

NINETEEN

Michael gripped the phone close to his mouth. "Hey, Dad, we are just about done here. I volunteered to stay for a few more operations so one of the guys could leave early; his wife is having a baby soon. It won't be long; I expect to be finished up in about a week. I'll also be helping to do turnover with the incoming team, then I'm headed out. My stuff is packed and ready to go."

"That's great news, Mikeys. Your mom and I can't wait to see you. We're going to celebrate and have a big party when you get back stateside." George felt great relief to learn that Michael was so close to coming home and almost silly for having thought that he may not see his son again. "Take care of yourself and we'll see you soon."

Michael hung up the satellite phone, returned it to the comm room, and headed over to the chow hall. Much like the rest of the buildings on Camp Corregidor, it was run by the 1st of the 506th. This deployment had been intense for both units. Fighting alongside each other day in and day out had cemented the bond between the two groups of men. The commander of the First, Lieutenant Colonel Ron Clark, had actually given the SEALs his battalion's patch, a black spade with a crimson number one positioned in the middle. The SEALs embraced their army counterparts and proudly wore the patch into battle. The army called the SEALs their "frogmen on the roof," and the men of SEAL Team 3 were eager to assist whenever their army brothers requested support.

A unit patch is a point of pride for many military personnel. Each unit is fairly particular about who they trade it with or present it to. But it is less common to be presented with one. Even so, receiving a member's unit patch represents a great deal of respect from one to the other, given or traded.

Michael finished his dinner and stood to clear his tray. As he walked to the other end of the hall, he saw Father Halladay enter. He gave him a quick head nod and big smile; they, too, had gotten to know each other well over the past six months. Michael would run over to Mass in the chapel whenever he found a chance and continued to stop in for confession in between operations. Oftentimes, he'd grab Rey to come over with him before they headed out. By this time, Rey had already left Camp Corregidor along with most of their platoon. Only eight SEALs from Delta remained to support any final operations that the army requested of the men.

The final operations had been a point of contention between the men in the platoon and their leaders, Doug Wallace recalls. Much of the equipment had been inventoried and packed onto pallets for shipment back to the US. In addition, the individual guys had packed most of their personal gear.

As the lead petty officer, he knew well that, for all intents and purposes, their work was done, and the men were ready to redeploy home. The army, however, was planning to conduct a few final operations and asked if the SEALs could support. Not all of the men would need to stay behind. Ultimately, the decision was left to the SEALs. Doug did not want to let their army brothers down and voiced his opinion that they should assist the battalion with sniper overwatch. "We owe it to them and ourselves to finish strong and support their mission," Doug had told the men as they all gathered in the hooch to discuss. Not all of the men agreed.

Preparations for redeployment had already been completed, but the leadership, including their platoon officer in charge, Seth Stone, felt it was important to be there to assist them.

The area where the SEALs were needed was rough; it was one of the most contested areas of the Malaab district. The enemy were well fortified and ready for a fight.

Much like earlier in the deployment when the platoon volunteered to move to Camp Corregidor, the men were asked, "Who would like to stay to support the army and conduct turnover operations?" From those who volunteered, eight were chosen, and the rest would begin movement back to the US. Michael remained and would be the automatic weapons gunner for one of the elements along with Mike Sarraille, Benny, and Doug.

September 27 was the first of the last two operations the SEALs were to support. The first operation was a success with fourteen enemies killed in action; however, it was not without risk. Doug and Benny narrowly missed being hit by enemy fire when a vehicle stopped nearby and an enemy fighter fired from the trunk of the car.[1] The round hit the lip of the wall where they were lying prone. It had become such a common occurrence that the SEALs began to expect effective enemy fire within thirty minutes upon entering the district. Even with the heavy firefight during that operation, all SEALs and army personnel returned back to camp safely.

It was the twenty-eighth of September and the 1st of the 506th had one last request: Operation Kentucky Jumper. The SEALs would be providing overwatch for Combat Outpost (COP) Eagle's Nest while the external wall of the COP was being reinforced. In addition, the 1st of the 506th would be conducting a clearance in the same area, which the SEALs would cover as well. The insert would take place at night. The two elements would leave COP Eagle's Nest and set up mutually supporting rooftop overwatch positions in two prominent houses much as they had been doing for the entire deployment. The men had conducted this type of operation many times, and at this point it seemed that this one would be much the same.

TWENTY

Michael looked down at his watch, "22:30, comms check in fifteen, ammo's good, water, extra batteries, all right, good to go." Michael walked over to the platoon communicator. "Hey, can I use the satellite phone real quick?" he asked.

"Sure, bro."

Michael dialed home, the phone began to ring: once, twice, three times . . . no answer. He listened to the message and after the beep, he said, "Hey, guys, it's Mike. Hello? Hello? Mom? Dad? . . . You'll be sorry you missed me. I'll catch you later," Michael added with a sound of disappointment.

Earlier that day the SEALs and their Iraqi partners had been dropped off at COP Eagle's Nest in preparation for the operation. The eight SEALs and the Iraqi scouts met at the gate of the COP. They checked each other over, made final preparations, and prepared to move.

"Doug, are we all good?" asked the lieutenant.

"We're good, point, lead us out."

It was dark. The crescent moon had just risen from the southwest horizon and would traverse the southern sky as the night passed. It would provide little help in illuminating the night for the insurgents, who lacked the technological capability to take advantage of the darkness, an advantage that the SEALs used with devastating results. Much as the Vietnam-era SEALs became known as the Men with Green Faces, special operators in the War on Terror would become known as the Men with Green Eyes. This was because of the faint green light from night vision optics that reflected off of the face of their user. Often the last thing seen by the enemy.

The operators moved silently through the Ramadi streets. From shadow to shadow, the men were careful of each step. The street was littered with trash and debris; one kicked can or bottle could compromise the patrol and alert the adversary. Although the residents of the city were used to gunfire and explosions, the population was constantly on edge. The early warning networks were efficient, and if the patrol was compromised, it could mean they would have to abort the operation. The group was split into two columns and patrolled across from each other on opposite sides of the street. This formation spread out the men and allowed each column to cover the other's high six, the angle above and behind an operator. The point element was comprised of the point man, two AW gunners, and an element leader. The rear of the element was similar in the event the patrol would have to be reversed. An enemy wishing to engage the group would have to not only choose a column leaving himself vulnerable to the other but also deal with the withering volume of fire from the AWs—dismal options for any aggressor. The target houses were not far from COP Eagle's Nest, about a mile, but this area was active and dangerous. Although they had done this numerous times over the past six months, a patrol through an urban environment was a stressful evolution. As he carefully moved through the streets, Michael scanned the buildings and houses around him. There were so many angles; it was impossible to cover them all.

"What if we were contacted right now? Where would I go? How can I best support my friends?" ran through Michael's head as the patrol moved closer to their objective.

This thought was constant, and it kept Michael focused and ready to act in a moment's notice. He continued to scan—no movement. The patrol was close, and Michael could see the turn onto the street that the target houses were on.

"Halt the patrol," came over the radio. From here, the two elements split and continued on to their respective target houses. Upon reaching the target, Michael took a security position looking down the road. Benny, Doug, and Mike Sarraille approached the door with the scouts.

The team quietly gained entry, and the scouts began to clear the house. Michael moved inside and joined the clearance. The house was secured, and the family was confined to one area. The scouts dealt with the family and held security on the first floor. The SEALs moved to the roof; Michael held security while the snipers and Mike S. began setting up the hide sites. It was around 4:00 a.m. when the men finished. They had found a few scraps of sheet metal and a barrel that they used in the setup in order to create shade and a benchrest.

The darkness began to give way to the rising sun, and the men could feel the temperature already beginning to climb. "It's going to be a hot one, guys," one of the SEALs remarked.

"Isn't it always?" Doug said.

The men laughed and continued to scan the area through their scopes. It was light enough now to see clearly at a distance. Michael had taken a position covering the road along with a row of houses that were to the backs of his teammates. An AW was very effective at stopping vehicles and covering larger areas with suppressive fire. Benny was facing to the east toward the other overwatch position to cover the other element's front door along with a large field that separated the two. Doug and Mike S. were next to each other facing into the city.

It was 7:00 a.m. and the army had just begun moving through the district. *Crack . . . crack . . . crack . . . crack.* The gunfire was coming from the direction of the clearance. Doug scanned; he knew the shots were close but could not see any movement. Then out from behind a house, a group of armed men began to maneuver in the direction of the army.

"I've got guys maneuvering with rifles," Doug called out. Michael moved quickly across the rooftop to Doug and Mike S.'s position. The three men engaged. Two of the insurgents went down immediately, and the others fled into the adjacent alleyway from where they had originally emerged. The men continued to search the area, sure that there would be a follow-up attack—if not on the army clearance team, on the overwatch, now that the enemy knew where the SEALs were.

Nothing came, though. The area was abnormally quiet. Michael stayed for a while just in case, but nothing. After some time, Doug turned to Michael. "Hey, bro, you want to hop on the gun for a bit?" referring to his Mk 11 sniper rifle, currently set up behind one of the loopholes.

"Yes, I do." Michael never turned down the chance if he got it. He was eager to learn whatever he could from the snipers in his platoon. Michael was set to attend the NSW sniper course after returning from deployment. This was not the first time he had taken a position behind one of these precision rifles. The men often rotated on and off the rifles to avoid scope fatigue, a condition that happens after looking through a magnified optic for an extended period. Blurred vision and headaches are the most common symptoms.

At around 11:00 a.m., the army moved out of the area having finished operations for the day. The SEAL overwatch positions remained in place and would extract under the cover of darkness later that night.

"Other than the 1st of the 506th doing clearance ops and us being in the area providing overwatch, it was kind of a somber day," Doug said, referring to how the day was going in comparison to other similar operations they had completed.

Based on most of the previous operations, the likelihood of another firefight was low. The temperature was reaching 115 degrees and would stay there until late into the afternoon and only begin to cool when the sun dipped below the horizon.

As the morning turned into day and then early afternoon, Michael, Doug, and Mike S. talked of heading home and what was next for each of the men.

"There was a sense of excitement. We were proud of what we did, we were proud of the relationships we had built with the army and the marine corps," recalls Mike Sarraille.

The men talked of their families. Doug would be headed to Georgia to see his three sons; Mike S. was ready to get back to his two-year-old little girl. Michael listened as the guys spoke of heading home. He was ready as well; sniper school, heading into his next platoon, snowboarding trips, and driving up the coast to see family in Garden Grove.

Doug recalls how cool and relaxed Michael was. "He just had a real calming sense to him. You could tell instantly what a great person and warrior he was." To this point, it was the most one-on-one time Doug had spent with Michael.

As the conversation continued, the men addressed a feeling they all shared. A strange feeling, a feeling that it was not yet time to return to normal life. There was still no recompense for Marc Lee and Ryan Job.

Task Unit Bruiser had been very successful in accomplishing their task for the deployment. Although Zarqawi had been killed in a targeted US bombing in June, his followers were still extremely active and controlled two-thirds of the city. The unified efforts of the soldiers, marines, and SEALs had not only disrupted but altogether halted the insurgent plan to make Ramadi the capital of the Muslim Caliphate in Iraq. The units had removed dozens of enemy fighters and their equipment from the battlefield. Still, the men could not shake the feeling.

Michael moved back to his original position looking down at the road and the row of houses. Still nothing to see on his side.

"Hey, guys, are you seeing this?" Benny called to the others.

He could see people setting up trash blockades that were blocking off the avenues of approach to the SEALs' position. This was new; the men had not seen this practice until now. It definitely got the guys' attention, but it was still benign enough to not be overly concerned about. Their position was elevated and far from where the blockade was being built.

As the day continued on, the intense heat had begun to wear on the men. The shade material helped, but the heat radiated from the surfaces all around them. Not even the light breeze brought reprieve. The air was stifling, dry, and filled with dust. The lack of activity and the heat induced lethargy, degrading the men's awareness.

Boom! An explosion rocked the rooftop. Michael ran back over to the position between Mike S. and Doug.

"What was that? RPG?" asked Doug.

"Sure seemed like it," Mike S. replied.

The anger on Michael's face was apparent as he searched for the insurgent responsible for the attack.

Mike S. moved out of his loophole and called the other element. "We just took an RPG. Searching for the shooter now. What have you guys got?"

Doug rolled into the open spot as it had a better field of view than his loophole. Michael sat on a chair between the two with his Mk 48 resting on the wall of the rooftop. Mike S. continued updating the other element while Michael, Doug, and Benny scanned the area. They saw nothing, no enemy movement.

Suddenly, an object just barely cleared the lip of the wall and hit Michael in the chest. It bounced off and rolled onto the ground directly in front of him. Mike S. looked over at what had just landed next to the group, then up at Michael. Michael stood so quickly and with such force that the chair he was sitting in sailed across the rooftop and impacted the opposite wall. Michael looked at Mike S. and yelled, "Grenade!"

Mike S. watched in disbelief as Michael, the only one of them who had an out to escape the blast, instead, lunged forward dropping directly onto the grenade.

The explosion was deafening. Blast and shrapnel smashed into Doug, Mike S., and Benny with such power that it flipped Mike S. onto his stomach and slammed Doug into the wall of the roof.

Mike S. turned his head back to where the blast had come from. Michael was lying facedown. "Mikey . . . Mikey . . . Mikey!" he yelled. The street below erupted with gunfire, which began to hit the edge of the rooftop. Benny was the first to reach Michael with Mike S. not far behind. They dragged Michael from the edge into the middle of the rooftop. Although wounded himself with shrapnel in his legs, Benny began to urgently assess Michael.

Mike S., badly wounded and in excruciating pain, tried to radio the other element. Hot metal shrapnel had passed through and remained lodged in his legs. He keyed up his radio, but nothing; it was dead. The blast wave had caused his radio to shut down. His head was pounding and his vision blurred. He looked around to see one of the partner force scouts lying curled against the wall. He remembered that they carried Motorola radios. Mike S. pushed himself up and tried to stand, but he couldn't walk and fell to the ground. Ultimately, he crawled over to the stunned scout and grabbed the radio. "Seth, this is Mike. Troops in contact, we need your help now . . . Mayday!"

Doug came to, not fully aware of what had happened. He could see Benny bent over Michael. His IFAK (Individual First Aid Kit) was open, and he was applying a chest seal to Michael's torso. He tried to move and felt searing pain throughout his entire body. He looked down to see blood covering his pants and his whole right side.

The enemy rounds continued hitting the wall and edges of the rooftop. Benny looked up from Michael. He could see both Doug and Mike S. were unable to stand. Medically, he had done all he could. Michael had taken the bulk of the blast and shrapnel; his wounds were many and grievous. With enemy gunfire increasing, Benny knew that if he didn't get back on a gun, none of them were going to make it off of the roof. He did not want to leave Michael's side, but this was the only thing left that he could do. Benny grabbed Michael's Mk 48 and went to work. He sent long continuous bursts back at the enemy. The pain from his wounds faded into rage.

By this point, the Iraqi scouts had made their way back onto the rooftop and began to help Benny with the fight guided by Doug and Mike S. The rooftop was taking heavy fire from multiple enemy automatic weapons. "Seth, you guys need to get here fast! Doug and I are hurt bad and Mikey is down hard," Mike S. called into the Motorola. He did not know that Seth and his team were already on the way to reach their position.

"Got you, we are coming. Hang in there, guys. The Bradleys are on the way," Seth called back in response.

Seth's element had heard and seen the two blasts from their overwatch position and were already moving when the call for help came in. The men urgently picked up the pace when they heard the amount of enemy automatic weapon fire that their friends were receiving. They broke out from the main entrance and headed west. Initially, all was quiet at their position, but within fifteen seconds of hitting the street, all hell broke loose. Enemy rounds snapped and skipped around them. They moved from cover to cover returning fire as they closed the distance to the other overwatch position.

They were only two blocks away, but to the wounded SEALs, it seemed like it took the other element forever to arrive.

"Hold on, Mikey, hold on, man," Mike S. said as he and Doug continued to assess and aid Michael.

Suddenly, a SEAL from the other element burst onto the roof and headed over to Doug, Mike S., and Michael. He was followed by Seth and the other SEALs. One of the strongest SEALs grabbed Michael and hoisted him onto his back. Seth grabbed Doug, and the others took Mike S. They could hear the 25-millimeter autocannons of the Bradley fighting vehicles begin to fire, effectively suppressing the enemy and providing cover for the SEALs to load their wounded. Mike S.

directed the group as they moved down the stairs and into the alley to the waiting Bradleys. Doug, Mike S., and Michael were loaded into the back along with one of the SEALs from the other element. He had stayed to continue to aid Michael while the Bradleys extracted them and headed back to Camp Corregidor.

When the wounded SEALs arrived, they saw the men from the 1st of the 506th lined up waiting to support wherever they could; another testament to the bond that the two units shared. Doug, Mike S., and Michael were loaded onto stretchers and brought into the aid station on the camp. Doug and Mike S. were given shots of morphine, and for the first time since the grenade explosion, they finally had reprieve from the piercing physical pain. The reprieve, however, was short lived. The atmosphere in the room shifted, the mood had darkened, and the two men could feel it. Then they overhead the nurse say it. Michael was gone. In that sobering moment, they became aware of what Michael had given them. He had freely exchanged his life for theirs.

It was September 29, the Feast Day of Saint Michael the Archangel, the protector and guide of warfighters since time immemorial and whom Michael had been named after twenty-five years earlier.

TWENTY-ONE

San Diego, California,
October 12, 2006

Doug leaned onto his crutches; his body throbbed. Just a few days earlier, dozens of tiny pieces of shrapnel had ripped through both of his legs and the right side of his body. He looked directly at George. It took everything he had to hold himself together. Doug cleared his throat. "I don't know what to say . . ." His voice shuttered and he stopped, his eyes still locked on George.

George looked back at him and answered with a strong but soft reply: "Just live a good life."

In the same area not far away, Mike Sarraille met Sally face-to-face for the first time. As his gaze met hers, he prepared to speak, but before he could utter a word, she hugged him as well as his two-year-old daughter and said, "I'm just so glad you are okay."

Her words sent a reverberation through his aching body. She had been through so much, yet she was concerned about him. He was awestruck by her selflessness.

George and Sally were in San Diego along with their children for the memorial service, funeral, and burial of their son. Guiding them throughout the events was Fr. Bill Petreska, a captain in the US Navy, whom they had personally chosen to be the celebrant at Michael's funeral. As Michael's closest friends stood up throughout the events to speak of the great man Michael was, they were still trying to process the reality that Michael was not coming home. Their deepest fear had been realized, and there were no words adequate to speak. So they barely did.

The culmination of all the events was when they arrived at Fort Rosecrans National Cemetery, a military cemetery on top of the cliffs of Point Loma in San Diego. It is situated in the middle of the peninsula that makes up Point Loma. It slopes gently to the west overlooking the San Diego Bay to the east and the great Pacific Ocean to the west. Its green fields are contrasted with the white rows of marble headstones, America's men and women in uniform who have come and gone. It is the final resting place for more than 120,000 of such men and women. The immaculate white rows are a powerful reminder, to any visitor, of the service and sacrifice that preserve their way of life. Michael had requested he be buried there should he pass away in battle. George and Sally honored those wishes and sat quietly beside each other while the burial ceremony transpired before their eyes.

As the ceremony neared completion, every SEAL stood up in formation and preceded to follow the pallbearers to Michael's final resting place. Almost every single SEAL on the West Coast was in attendance. Without a word, the men began to walk solemnly side by side to Michael's casket. It was not clear to any of the other people in attendance what the men were doing. *Thump!* The sound echoed through the cemetery. *Thump!* and again *Thump!* This continued over and over for twenty minutes, each time sending a resounding echo into the rows of headstones around the scene.

One by one, each SEAL approached Michael's casket, removed his trident, carefully placed it, and slammed its pins into the wood. The trident is the warfare pin that new SEALs receive upon completion and graduation of UDT/SEAL training. It is what delineates them as special warfare operators within the US Navy. Gold in color, it is the only warfare pin in the navy that is gold for both enlisted sailors and officers due to the selection process that places both side by side as they endure the rigors of training together as equals. The warfare pin consists of an eagle bowing its head with an anchor in the middle. In its talons, the eagle grips a cocked flintlock pistol and a trident. The eagle represents the air and a SEAL's proficiency in airborne operations, its head bowed in humility and respect for the warfighters of the past. The anchor represents birth from and continued service in the US Navy. The trident represents Poseidon or Neptune, the god of the sea and the deep connection a SEAL has with the ocean. The pistol signifies a SEAL's ability with weapons of war, its hammer cocked, ready at a moment's notice.

The act was one final gesture of honor and respect for their brother in arms. SEAL after SEAL followed. The top of Michael's casket as well as much of the sides had been gilded and were now shining brightly in the sunlight. The actions of those men put into common practice a tradition that continues to this day at SEAL operator burials.

TWENTY-TWO

The bow cut through the ocean's swells effortlessly as sixteen-foot waves beat against the steel hull of the massive warship. Inside, the effects of the storm could barely be felt by her crew. For untold millennia, man has battled the ocean for the privilege of sailing atop its briny depths. Now here, almost two and a half centuries after the first US warships took up the fight, the perpetual struggle continues. But just as the crew aboard this ship would be helpless without her, so it is for the ship without her crew. For neither can stand alone against such power as is the ocean and its depths.

Only hours after having left the Kennebec River and sailing out of the Gulf of Maine, the Zumwalt-class warship was now off the coast of Cape Cod, Massachusetts. Captain Scott Smith was on the bridge as the meteorological reports came in. The captain looked at his watch: "22:30, watches are set, condition zebra set. Okay, we are ready," he thought as he looked out toward the approaching storm. At 23:00, it hit. The storm produced massive swells, sixteen-foot waves, and winds in excess of ninety miles per hour. The spray coming off the bow was swept up by the wind causing zero visibility, a devastating prospect for many ships on the sea. The wind and waves beat against the ship in vain. Because of its mass and the shape of her bow, she cut through all of it unfazed, but she did not do it alone. Within her hull, man and machine worked in unison to combat the storm. The men and women aboard worked quickly and diligently to ensure the ship continued on and her systems were functioning as intended. Captain Smith observed them executing their tasks with satisfaction and a sense of pride, his eyes now affixed to the screens and instruments before him. This massive guided-missile destroyer was barely fazed by the elemental assault that lasted through the night. At daybreak, the storm had passed, and although the seas were still heavy, the ship continued smoothly toward her destination.

The ship and her crew sailed south down the East Coast of the US past Florida, Cuba, Colombia, and into the Panama Canal. Because of its mammoth size, having a width of eighty-one feet and the canal locks being at 110 feet, the ship only had a clearance of fourteen-and-a-half feet on each side, which made for a tight journey through the canal. The ship continued south into the Gulf of Panama, then west and finally northwest and onto its final destination, the San Diego Harbor.

It was early morning, the swells of the Pacific Ocean rolling just slightly against the bow as the ship cut through the water. The sun was glistening off the surface of the ocean with not a cloud in the sky. A normal San Diego day in Southern California, but it was not a normal day for the sailors of DDG-1001. Before the ship would enter the San Diego Bay and on into the harbor, Captain Smith and the crew had one more task to do. He had given his crew instructions days prior. The sailors prepared their dress blue uniforms and waited for the order.

From the bridge, the crew could see the city of San Diego. Normally, preparations to enter the mouth of the bay would begin, but in this case, there were no such preparations. Instead, the crew were busy donning their dress uniforms and checking each other over. The ship passed the entrance to the bay, steamed a few more miles north, then made a sweeping turn back to the south. Captain Smith brought the ship close to the Southern California shore. Every crew member not absolutely essential for ship function assembled on deck and manned the rails in full dress uniform. The ship was quickly approaching Point Loma. Suddenly, a whistle blew, and in unison, the crew lifted their right hand and saluted as they sailed past the Rosecrans Cemetery atop Point

Loma directly abeam the ship. It was over in a moment but had monumental meaning to each crew member aboard, especially Captain Smith.

Once they passed the cemetery, the ship turned into the San Diego Bay and headed for the 32nd Street harbor. This would be the ship's new home port where it would be commissioned and officially brought to life by the US Navy in the following days, a tradition dating back to 1775.[1] The time and effort it took for this ship to arrive at its home port was not lost on any of the men and women who assisted in its creation, construction, christening, sailing, and now, finally, commissioning. The ship had been inscribed with its sponsor's initials and given an identity and spirit of its own after its namesake in the years leading up to this point. Now, it was time to officially bring the ship to life.

January 26, 2019

The dignitaries approached the stage one by one: revered army and naval officers, congressmen, retired veterans, distinguished guests, the only woman among them, the ship's sponsor, and finally Captain Smith. The ship's crew stood proudly at the back of the audience, anxious and ready, standing by to receive orders. The executive officer, Captain Jim Edwards, the emcee for the ceremony, welcomed everyone in attendance. A grateful and excited crowd filled the pier at Naval Air Station North Island in Coronado, California.

Major Halladay was announced and approached the podium to give the invocation. He had flown in all the way from Korea for this special event. Upon finishing his opening prayer, the other speakers approached the podium. One after the other they rendered their special remarks and honored the family of the ship's namesake as well as the impressive ship itself.[2]

Then, Major General Ron Clark, who led the 1st of the 506th "Red Currahee" Battalion during the Battle of Ramadi, walked commandingly over to the podium. "'We few, we happy few, we band of brothers; For he to-day [who shares] his blood with me shall be my brother.' The bravery and sacrifice of these warriors is the highest form of service to our nation. At a time when less than 1 percent of American citizens will ever don the cloth of our nation in her defense, these men and women endured hardship, danger, and personal sacrifice every day to protect our country and our way of life. Let me be very clear, our band of brothers was brought together through our fight against a tough and violent enemy . . . in fact, we refer to SEAL Team 3 as Army SEALs. . . . It was the fight that brought us together, but really, what defined our task force was one word, love. A brotherly love that warriors-in-arms share in battle, defined by selfless commitment to a mission, and selfless commitment unfailing to one another. There is no greater human emotion than the feeling to belong: to a team, to a unit, to a brotherhood, to a family. My associations with these warriors . . . have been the most meaningful professional relationships of my life."

When the last of the distinguished speakers had finished, Captain Smith stepped forward. To this point, he had spent countless hours and months preparing for this moment, an event that he intricately planned and set into motion with his loyal crew. He glanced backward toward Admiral Moran, the vice chief of Naval Operations, and said, "Admiral Moran, we'd be honored if you would now place [our ship] in commission."

Admiral Moran stood up and leaned forward and spoke clearly into the microphone for all to hear: "On behalf of the secretary of the Navy and for the president of the United States, I hereby place United States Ship . . . in commission. May God bless and guide this warship and all who shall sail in her."

Captain Smith then issued the first order as the commander of this newly commissioned ship: "Executive officer, hoist the colors and the commission pennant."

Captain Jim Edwards then ordered the quartermaster to hoist the colors and the commission pennant. This has been a tradition with professional navies since the seventeenth century. Naval ships used them to distinguish themselves from merchant ships. For the US Navy, it's a long, narrow streamer with one row of seven stars and red over white horizontal stripes.[3]

The crowd was asked to stand as the quartermaster hoisted the American flag and pennant hand over hand until it swayed gently on top of the deckhouse where it will fly continuously until the ship is decommissioned.

"Admiral Moran, United States Ship . . . is in commission and I am in command. Executive officer, set the watch," Captain Smith stated.

"Aye, aye, sir," responded the executive officer, Captain Edwards. He continued, "In days of sail, the boatswain's mate would call forth the watch; today the sound of boatswain's pipes still pierces the air to make major announcements. . . . The officer on deck is the commanding officer's direct representative. While on watch, [he] is responsible for the safe operation of the ship and the crew. The long glass is the traditional symbol of the officer's authority in a ship of the line."

Michael's brothers, Jim and Joe, stood up and carried the symbolic golden long glass and presented it to 2nd Class Petty Officer Jorge Cordona. He replied, "Sir, the watch is set."

Jorge and his three fellow petty officers marched forward to take their positions aboard the ship.

Finally, the ship's sponsor and sole woman on the stage arose and walked to the podium. She smiled, her humble demeanor evident to all in attendance. She began by sharing her heartfelt gratitude to all who were with them today to honor her son. She continued, thanking the men and women of the military whom she regarded as the best in the world. Finally, and without further ado, she gave the order that the crew had been eagerly waiting to hear: "Officers and crew of the USS *Michael Monsoor*, man our ship and bring her to life."

A loud and in unison "Aye, aye, ma'am," was the reply from the waiting crew and echoed through the harbor.

Sally Monsoor took a deep breath. She knew she must keep her composure. She watched as the crew members ran from their position in the formation, "Anchors Aweigh" playing in the background. They approached side by side down the aisle splitting left and right only feet away from her as she stood at the front of the stage. Each crew member then ran up the gangway to man her son's ship.

Sally was overcome with memories. They flashed through her mind in what felt like an instant: Michael as a small boy with his brother Jim in their little red matching overalls, when he had run away from her in the mall and was brought back, a mischievous smile on his face, by the security guard. Michael flying down the hilly sidewalk in his homemade boxcar, arms raised high and eyes lit up with glee. Michael racing his siblings in the pool, Michael grinning at her as he urged his Corvette to go faster and faster, Michael in full uniform smiling so proudly as he became a US Navy SEAL. Dancing with his grandmother, riding the train with her and George to Santa Barbara, hugging her goodbye, laughing, smiling, crying, kissing his forehead . . . it was all rushing back.

She was overcome with emotion but continued to stand up straight and composed. She was so proud in that moment and then, behind the crew, she recognized familiar faces as they began to run up the aisle toward her. Michael's teammates . . . the men he last fought beside and had given his life protecting. They were the men of Task Unit Bruiser and the 1st of the 506th. The same brothers-in-arms Michael had gone to war alongside were now helping bring his ship to life. It was almost more than she could bear, and yet her strength did not fail.

"Ladies and gentlemen, the crew of the USS *Michael Monsoor* salutes you! We are proud to serve in your great navy. Captain, USS *Michael Monsoor* is manned and ready," stated Captain Edwards, as the crew stood at attention lining the deck of the ship from bow to stern while its flags waved, both in full regalia.

Sally's memories continued . . . welding her and George's initials into the keel, meeting the shipbuilders, sealing the wooden box during the mast stepping ceremony, breaking the champagne bottle upon the bow, gifting a Saint Michael statue to the crew, and now, bringing her son's ship to life.

———

Father Halladay stepped up to the podium. "Let us pray. Heavenly Father, bless and approve this newly commissioned vessel, the USS *Michael Monsoor* and its crew. Send your holy angels as custodians and guides. May

Michael the Archangel ever defend it in battle. Be its protector against all enemies and ravages of foul weather. May this vessel and crew always know the friendship of the creatures of the deep, the comradery of the winds, and the amenity of the tides. And may the USS *Michael Monsoor* ever know the unified patronage of the citizens of heaven, the creatures of the earth, and every mission it undertakes: to restore peace, ensure freedom, and enact justice for all. Amen."

MA2 (SEAL) Michael Monsoor had completed his watch in the defense of others, and now, the USS *Michael Monsoor* began hers, carrying with her a legacy that he so honorably left behind.

AWARDS

Michael Anthony Monsoor (April 5, 1981–September 29, 2006) received the Medal of Honor posthumously for his actions on September 29, 2006. President George W. Bush presented the medal to his parents, George and Sally, at the White House on April 8, 2008. The Medal of Honor is the highest award in the United States for military valor in action. It was created in the 1860s specifically for "non-commissioned officers and privates as shall most distinguish themselves by their gallantry in action, and other soldier-like qualities" during the American Civil War.[1] Now, over a century and a half later, the meaning behind the Medal remains untarnished and the current criteria for being awarded is as follows:

The Medal is authorized for any military service member who "distinguishes himself conspicuously by gallantry and intrepidity at the risk of his life above and beyond the call of duty while engaged in an action against an enemy of the United States."

Michael's full military citation is found below.

The President of the United States in the name of The Congress takes pride in presenting the MEDAL OF HONOR posthumously to

MASTER-AT-ARMS SECOND CLASS (SEA, AIR AND LAND)
MICHAEL A. MONSOOR
UNITED STATES NAVY

for service as set forth in the following

CITATION:

For conspicuous gallantry and intrepidity at the risk of his life above and beyond the call of duty while serving as an Automatic Weapons Gunner for Naval Special Warfare Task Group Arabian Peninsula, during the Battle of Ramadi, Iraq, on 29 September 2006. As a member of a combined SEAL and Iraqi Army sniper overwatch team, he was tasked with providing early warning and stand-off protection in support of Task Force Red Currahee in an insurgent held sector of Ramadi. Petty Officer Monsoor distinguished himself by his exceptional bravery in the face of grave danger and a determined enemy. In the early morning, enemy insurgents began to execute a coordinated assault on the team's rooftop position. Snipers thwarted the enemy's initial attack by killing two insurgents, but the enemy continued to assault, engaging the team with a rocket-propelled grenade and effective small-arms fire. Despite the increase in enemy activity, Petty Officer Monsoor and his team refused the idea of abandoning their position, which at this point provided crucial protection for the western flank of American troops. He took up a position with his machine gun between two teammates on an outcropping of the roof, from which the three SEALs were able to maximize their coverage of the area most vulnerable to enemy attack. While the SEALs vigilantly watched for enemy movement, an insurgent threw a hand grenade from an unseen location, which bounced off Petty Officer Monsoor's chest and landed in front of him. He instantly identified the immediate danger to his teammates, who were located just feet from the grenade. Although he could have escaped the blast, he instead chose to protect his fellow SEALs. Unhesitatingly, and with complete disregard for his own life, he threw himself onto the grenade, and absorbed the force of the explosion with his body, saving the lives of two teammates and preventing probable injury to another. Petty Officer Monsoor's undaunted courage, selfless nature, and unwavering devotion to duty in the face of certain death reflect great credit upon himself and are in keeping with the highest traditions of the United States Naval Service. He gallantly gave his life for his country.

Michael also received a Silver Star for his actions on May 9, 2006, where he saved the life of his wounded SEAL teammate while under heavy enemy fire. The Silver Star is the third-highest military combat decoration that can be awarded to a member of the United States Armed Forces for gallantry in action.[2]

Michael's full military citation is found below.

THE SECRETARY OF THE NAVY
WASHINGTON, D.C. 20350-1000

The President of the United States takes pride in presenting the SILVER STAR MEDAL posthumously to

MASTER-AT-ARMS SECOND CLASS (SEA, AIR AND LAND)
MICHAEL A. MONSOOR
UNITED STATES NAVY

for service as set forth in the following

CITATION:

For conspicuous gallantry and intrepidity in action against the enemy as Platoon Machine Gunner, Naval Special Warfare Task Group — Arabian Peninsula, Task Unit Ramadi, Iraq on 9 May 2006. Petty Officer Monsoor was the Platoon Machine Gunner of an overwatch element, providing security for an Iraqi Army Brigade during counter-insurgency operations. While moving toward extraction, the Iraqi Army and Naval Special Warfare overwatch team received effective enemy automatic weapons fire resulting in one SEAL wounded in action. Immediately, Petty Officer Monsoor, with complete disregard for his own safety, exposed himself to heavy enemy fire in order to provide suppressive fire and fight his way to the wounded SEAL's position. He continued to provide effective suppressive fire while simultaneously dragging the wounded SEAL to safety. Petty Officer Monsoor maintained suppressive fire as the wounded SEAL received tactical casualty treatment to his leg. He also helped load his wounded teammate into a High Mobility Multi-Purpose Wheeled Vehicle for evacuation, then returned to combat. By his bold initiative, undaunted courage, and complete dedication to duty, Petty Officer Monsoor reflected great credit upon himself and upheld the highest traditions of the United States Naval Service.

For the President,

Secretary of the Navy

In addition, Michael received a Bronze Star with Valor, which is awarded for heroic achievement in a combat zone. The "V" device is worn on decorations to denote valor, an act or acts of heroism by an individual above what is normally expected while engaged in direct combat with an enemy of the United States with exposure to enemy hostilities and personal risk.[3]

Michael's full military citation is found below.

COMMANDER
NAVAL SPECIAL WARFARE COMMAND

The President of the United States takes pleasure in presenting the **BRONZE STAR MEDAL** posthumously to

MASTER-AT-ARMS SECOND CLASS (SEA, AIR AND LAND)
MICHAEL A. MONSOOR
UNITED STATES NAVY

for service as set forth in the following

CITATION:

For heroic achievement in connection with combat operations against the enemy as Task Unit Ramadi, Iraq, Combat Advisor for Naval Special Warfare Task Group - Arabian Peninsula in support of Operation IRAQI FREEDOM from April to September 2006. On 11 different operations, Petty Officer Monsoor exposed himself to heavy enemy fire while shielding his teammates with suppressive fire. He aggressively stabilized each chaotic situation with focused determination and uncanny tactical awareness. Each time insurgents assaulted his team with small arms fire or rocket propelled grenades, he quickly assessed the situation, determined the best course of action to counter the enemy assaults, and implemented his plan to gain the best tactical advantage. His selfless, decisive, heroic actions resulted in 25 enemy killed and saved the lives of his teammates, other Coalition Forces and Iraqi Army soldiers. By his extraordinary guidance, zealous initiative, and total dedication to duty, Petty Officer Monsoor reflected great credit upon himself and upheld the highest traditions of the United States Naval Service.

The Combat Distinguishing Device is authorized.

For the President,

J. Maguire

J. MAGUIRE
Rear Admiral, United States Navy
Commander, Naval Special Warfare Command

Finally, he received the following awards for his combined actions throughout his deployment to Ramadi as well as exceptionalism in the performance of his duties as a Navy SEAL:

Purple Heart | Combat Action Ribbon | Navy Good Conduct Medal | National Defense Service Medal | Iraq Campaign Medal | Global War on Terror Service Medal | Sea Service Deployment Ribbon | Navy and Marine Corps Overseas Service Ribbon | Navy Expert Rifle | Navy Expert Pistol

MEMORIALS

Michael has been honored nationwide for his selfless actions in defense of his brothers in arms. Following is a list of current memorials:

Dr. Donald C. Winter, former secretary of the Navy and author of the foreword, chose to name DDG Zumwalt Class 1001 after Michael A. Monsoor and selected Sally, his mother, to be the ship's sponsor. San Diego, California

SEAL Team 3 Quarterdeck, Coronado, California

Mount Soledad National Veteran's Memorial, La Jolla, California

Mountain Warfare Training Camp Michael Monsoor, Campo, California

Michael A. Monsoor Memorial Stadium, Garden Grove, California

Michael Monsoor Ct., Garden Grove, California

The Currahee Memorial at Fort Campbell, Kentucky

Michael A. Monsoor Sea Cadet Battalion, Pendleton,
California

National Corvette Museum, Bowling Green, Kentucky

Holy Trinity Catholic Church, Norfolk, Virginia

Perhaps some of the most meaningful memorials in his honor, however, are the young men living today who have been named in his memory. His younger brother, Joe, has a young Mikey who was baptized in the bell of the USS *Michael Monsoor* by Father Halladay in a tradition that originated centuries prior in the Royal British Navy. In doing so, the belief is that the act symbolizes an invisible tie created between the United States of America, the ship, and its citizens.[1]

Mike Sarraille told Sally that if he ever had a son, he would name him Michael, and Sally responded, "Well, it's a good thing your name is Michael."

He insisted that it would not be for him but to honor Mikey. And sure enough, when he became a father to his son a few years later, he named him Michael Anthony Sarraille.

Scott Reynolds gave his son the middle name Michael after his good friend Mike who is affectionately remembered as "Uncle Mike" in their household.

Chris H. also has a son named Michael in remembrance of his dear friend and credits his conversion to Catholicism in thanks to Michael and their many conversations about faith during their time together in Sicily. Michael Monsoor's brother Joe is young Michael's godfather.

REMEMBRANCE

Michael was made an honorary chief by the US Navy in thanks to efforts by Captain Smith and Master Chief Pat Tummins. He was also inducted as an honorary member of the 1st of the 506th, the first navy sailor to do so in the army battalion's eighty-plus-year history.

Captain Smith and his crew made it a point to visit Michael's grave on the tenth anniversary of his death, on September 29, 2016. They gathered in San Diego at Fort Rosecrans with Sally and some of her family along with Doug Wallace. There, they placed flowers as well as a piece of the "keel block," which was what the ship rested on during the construction phase.

Captain Smith recalls the memorable day: "In Bath, the crew held a small ceremony and placed a wreath into the Kennebec River, and in Norfolk, some of the crew gathered with Rey Baviera. We shared these various moments with Sally so that she knew the entire crew had stopped to honor Mike. That day created one of the most vivid memories I have of my entire time with the Monsoor family and the ship. As the ceremony at Fort Rosecrans ended and the crew was filing out, Sally leaned over and kissed the gravestone, like any parent would kiss the forehead of their child, and it left a mark in the upper right corner of Michael's gravestone, which remains to this day. That is the image I will carry with me, and it was that act that inspired the crew to work so hard to honor Mike, his family, and his teammates."

George and his family along with his teammates and friends continue to visit Michael's gravestone, where it is almost never without a cigar, coins, an American flag, or flowers. He is gone but will never be forgotten.

ACKNOWLEDGMENTS

We would like to thank all of the incredible men who shared their personal stories about Michael for this biography. Your lives have been lived in protection of others and being able to listen to your unique stories was most edifying. Thank you for your support and trust. Michael chose to surround himself with top-notch friends, and it shows. Gabe Lynch, Mike Sarraille, Doug Wallace, Z., Scott Reynolds, Rey Baviera, Chris Kimbrell, Dale Fortin, Jocko Willink, Leif Babin, J. P. Dinnell, Kevin Lacz, Chris Holuka, Ali Atash-Sobh, Father Paul Halladay, and Tom Deshazo. This story would have never been possible without you.

To Brent West of Bath Iron Works, thank you for sharing the expansive ship information; it was fascinating.

To Captain Scott Smith, thank you for your service and impeccable memory and efforts to honor Michael and his life. Thank you also for your assistance with the ship chapters and Michael's awards, memorials, and photos.

To the US Navy, the "Aci boys," Michael Fumento, and Michael's BUD/S Class and teammates, especially Rey Baviera, Gabe Lynch, and Doug Wallace, who shared your incredible photos of Michael, thank you!

To Steve Gilmore, you are a light to so many and a vital part of this project. Thank you for your service to our nation, Naval Special Warfare, and all families of the fallen and in need. You have guided and connected so many of us.

Finally, to the publishing and production team that contributed their talent and resources to bring this project to fruition, we are so grateful: Meaghan Porter, senior editor at Harper Horizon, Andrea Fleck-Nisbet, publisher at Harper Horizon, Belinda Bass, creative director at HarperCollins, Dave McNeill, copyeditor, and Jeff Farr, production editor, Neuwirth & Associates.

To my wife, children, and grandchildren. To the SEALs and the men who served with my son Michael.

—GEORGE MONSOOR

I would like to dedicate this passion project to George and Sally Monsoor as well as all defenders who serve our great country. May generation after generation understand what was fought and paid for in blood and sacrifice. To my husband, Ryan, graduate of BUD/S class 251, who sat beside me for countless hours and used his experience and articulation to bring the stories from Michael's life alive for the readers. Finally, to Our Lady of Victory and Saint Michael the Archangel, may you continue through the Grace of God to guide and protect righteous warfighters for ages to come.

—ROSE REA

NOTES

Chapter Five

1. "The Legacy of Admiral Elmo R. Zumwalt Jr.," Naval History and Heritage Command, January 5, 2022, https://www.history .navy.mil/browse-by-topic/people/chiefs-of-naval-operations /admiral-elmo-r--zumwalt-jr-/zumwalt-legacy.html.

2. "Destroyers (DDG-1000)," America's Navy, updated April 27, 2021, https://www.navy.mil/Resources/Fact-Files/Display -FactFiles/article/2391800/destroyers-ddg-1000/.

3. Colin Darlington, "The Significance of Keel Laying," The Maritime Executive, October 14, 2018, https://www.maritime -executive.com/blog/the-significance-of-keel-laying.

Chapter Six

1. "The Faraglioni of Aci Trezza (Sicily) and the Legend of Polyphemus," *Italy* magazine, n.d., https://www.italymagazine .com/dual-language/faraglioni-aci-trezza-sicily-and-legend -polyphemus.

Chapter Ten

1. USS *Michael Monsoor* Commissioning Book.

2. "USS *Constitution* Timeline," USS *Constitution* Museum, 2022, https://ussconstitutionmuseum.org/discover-learn/history /timeline/.

Chapter Thirteen

1. Columnist Richard Grenier, *Insight on the News*, May 3, 1993.

Chapter Seventeen

1. "Michael Monsoor Legacy" by Joshua Furnish.

Chapter Nineteen

1. "The Last Mission - Remembering Michael Monsoor," *Truth and Tribe with Mike Sarraille* (podcast), Truth+ Media, https://www .truthplusmedia.com/truth-plus-tribe/everyday-warrior-alrt9 -eshp3-3362t-8zhsr-7l78l-hyspx-jdbbl-x4ggh-64kmh.

Chapter Twenty-Two

1. "Ship Launching and Commissioning," Naval History and Heritage Command, April 23, 2019, https://www.history.navy .mil/browse-by-topic/heritage/customs-and-traditions0/ship -launching-and-commissioning.html.

2. Quotes in this chapter taken from the USS *Michael Monsoor* Ship Commissioning Video, https://www.youtube.com/watch?v =7ehuzHmWn4A.

3. "Commissioning Pennant," Naval History and Heritage Command, April 19, 2018, https://www.history.navy.mil/browse -by-topic/heritage/customs-and-traditions0/ship-launching -and-commissioning.html.

Awards

1. Congressional Medal of Honor Society, https://www.cmohs .org/.

2. Military Awards for Valor, US Department of Defense, valor .defense.gov.

3. Air Force Personnel Center, https://www.afpc.af.mil.

Memorials

1. "Ships' Bells," Naval History and Heritage Command, February 2, 2018, https://www.history.navy.mil/research/library/online -reading-room/title-list-alphabetically/b/bells-on-ships.html.

ABOUT THE AUTHORS

GEORGE MONSOOR is Michael's father and a Marine veteran. He was born in Wisconsin and moved to Southern California at an early age. George and his late wife, Sally, were married for forty-nine years and have four children, including Michael, along with nine grandchildren. He has spent more than five decades in the business and entrepreneurial fields and continues to reside in Southern California.

ROSE REA has worked with high-end regional and national publications for fifteen years, including founding her own, which she has since sold. She is also the creator of the coffee-table book *Spirit and Life*. She is a SEAL wife and mother of six children.